Praise for *Racism a*

"You have never read anything like *Racism as Zoological Witchcraft*, which draws on history, critical race theory, and pop culture to make compelling arguments about the impact of white supremacy both on race and our treatment of animals, especially given the dehumanizing nature of racism. Partially informed by Jordan Peele's *Get Out*, but drawing on a wide variety of research, Aph Ko helps us envision a world beyond our limited notions of 'intersectionality' to chart a course for a more humane future."
—**Tananarive Due**, author, *Freedom in the Family: A Mother–Daughter Memoir of the Struggle for Civil Rights*

"*Racism as Zoological Witchcraft* is a sophisticated throwdown about how we can re-think anti-racist and animal rights activism(s) in a modality more nearly adequate to our profound entanglement in white supremacy's comprehensive and hydra-headed monstrosity. Liquefying arcane academic theory in popular culture fluidity, Aph Ko offers a voice at once critical, generous, and polysemous. Her Afro-futurism relentlessly tracks the racialized animality of white cannibalism that eludes 'sighting' in discrete discourses and intersectional advocacies. The multi-dimensional liberation she conjures demands a political hearing from anyone laboring for a different future."—**James W. Perkinson**, professor of Social Ethics and Theology, Ecumenical Theological Seminary

"*Racism as Zoological Witchcraft* is a fascinating, groundbreaking, thoughtful work that shows nuanced relationships between systems that historically dehumanize people of color and the consumption of animals as food. This transformative framework is as disturbing as it is enlightening. Aph Ko steadfastly demonstrates that veganism can be more than a matter of health and lifestyle—that plant-based diets can be a radical practice in valuing the aligned rights of all living beings on Earth as well as a practice in dismantling systems on our planet that devalue humanity."—**Ytasha L. Womack**, author, *Afrofuturism: The World of Black Sci Fi & Fantasy Culture*

"*Racism as Zoological Witchcraft* is an exciting hands-on theoretical guide to white supremacy's grounding in 'zoological racism,' a violent devouring of the bodies, souls, and lives of all it deems 'animal,' both nonhuman and human. This 'guide to getting out' also illustrates the dangers of supposedly liberatory movements that do not recognize 'the animal' as the source of violence against animals *as well as* black people, ultimately providing its readers with the intellectual tools to imagine and enact 'afro-zoological resistance' and liberation for *all*—what could be more important or inspiring?!"—**Lindgren Johnson**, author, *Race Matters, Animal Matters: Fugitive Humanism in African America, 1840–1930*

"Aph Ko's brilliant analysis on zoological racism and movement politics is transformative, challenging everything readers think they understand about racism. By framing white supremacy as a zoological witchcraft practice, she cuts across genres and offers something completely new, linking race and animals in a powerful book that is sure to wake readers up." —**lauren Ornelas**, Executive Director, Food Empowerment Project

"In *Racism as Zoological Witchcraft*, Aph Ko has written an accessible argument rooted in theory that is eminently readable and will have broad appeal. In her argument for what she calls 'epistemic ruptures,' Ko has created a compelling treatise against making current activist movements merge, arguing instead that our conception of 'the animal,' as a label for consumable and disposable bodies, is tied to the legacy of racism that operates by virtue of zoological, white supremacist witchcraft. Using examples from popular culture—including Jordan Peele's 2017 film *Get Out*—Ko examines the tension that exists between contemporary anti-racism and animal rights movements and argues for an examination of 'raw' oppressions that can move the conversation beyond modern day liberation movements in ways that intersectionality has been unable to achieve.—**Laura Wright**, author, *The Vegan Studies Project: Food, Animals, and Gender in the Age of Terror*

"Aph Ko's work is at the center of a conceptual Big Bang. Theorizing beyond increasingly stale notions like diversity, speciesism, and intersectionality, she takes us back to the 'raw oppression' itself. She guides our hands towards the one weapon that has characterized every true movement against oppression: recognizing the incomplete nature of our current justice movements. The scholarship is as rigorous as it is accessible and refreshingly inspiring. Her insights not only challenge all of us concerned with racial and animal oppression to imagine new pathways forward, but to recognize that much of Black thought from Frederick Douglass to Angela Davis already had gone beyond a vision of racial justice or human dignity to open toward a vision of freedom for all life."—**Aaron S. Gross**, associate professor, University of San Diego, and founder of Farm Forward

RACISM AS ZOOLOGICAL WITCHCRAFT

A GUIDE TO GETTING OUT

APH KO

Lantern Books ● Brooklyn, NY

2019
Lantern Books
128 2nd Place
Brooklyn, NY 11231
www.lanternbooks.com

Copyright © 2019 Aph Ko

Illustrations: © Alise and Jack Eastgate
Film stills from *Get Out*: © Universal Pictures/Photofest

Printed in the United States of America.

Library of Congress Cataloging-in-Publication Data

Names: Ko, Aph, author.
Title: Racism as zoological witchcraft : a guide to getting out / Aph Ko.
Description: Brooklyn : Lantern Books, [2019].
Identifiers: LCCN 2019014095 (print) | LCCN 2019980316 (ebook) |
    ISBN 9781590565964 (paperback) | ISBN 9781590565971 (ebook other)
Subjects: LCSH: Racism—Philosophy. | Intersectionality (Sociology) |
    Feminist theory. | Veganism—Philosophy.
Classification: LCC HT1521 .K54 2019 (print) | LCC HT1521 (ebook) |
    DDC 305.8001—dc23
LC record available at https://lccn.loc.gov/2019014095
LC ebook record available at https://lccn.loc.gov/2019980316

African Americans, I argue, were animal agents long before animal rights or even animal welfare movements existed in the United States, and their perspectives are essential to understanding the full scope of thinking on both human and animal liberation.
—**Lindgren Johnson** (2018, 140)

With white supremacist practice . . . we do know that the flesh is consumed (in slave and wage labor), and we know how it is secured (by military force, institutional discrimination, cultural normalization, etc.). . . . Whiteness, under the veneer of its "heavenly" pallor, is a great grinding witch tooth, sucking blood and tearing flesh without apology. . . .
—**James W. Perkinson** (2004, 622–3)

Contents

FOREWORD

SOMETIMES A BOOK COMES ALONG THAT HAS THE POTENTIAL TO CHANGE how people think. This is one of those books. *Racism as Zoological Witchcraft* does more than break new ground—it takes the ground we thought we knew, the ground beneath our feet, and shows us with bracing clarity that it isn't as solid as we thought. Poised at the juncture between race studies and animal studies, Aph Ko's book makes a brilliant intervention in both—beginning with the way it bluntly interrogates the separation between the two. Ko asks: What is race studies if it does not contend with the animal? What is animal studies if it does not contend with race? Are these two separate subjects of inquiry or one subject that has been falsely split in two?

To appreciate Ko's intervention, we might consider where race studies and animal studies have been lately. Race studies has, for the most part, been putting up every manner of fencing to keep (the question of) the animal out. Part of this is ordinary disciplinary territoriality—minding property lines, keeping order, fending off critters that might reduce the crop yield. But perhaps the larger part, as Ko suggests, is a restless anxiety about acknowledging a relation whose deployment has been central to the abjection of racialized populations and the justification of their torture, enslavement, and eradication. White supremacy has been so keen on animalizing nonwhites for the past many centuries, has made such productive use of this association, that it has perhaps seemed the safer course for race studies to denounce the association and push it out of sight—rather than exploring the terrifying space of abjection that binds together racialized peoples and animalized creatures.

Animal studies, for its part, has been scarcely less resistant to talking about race. Now "speciesism" has been analogized to racism from the start (the better to borrow the latter's *gravitas*), and conferences and anthologies in the field increasingly make room for discussions of race, so, in a superficial sense, the field has always talked about race, and perhaps now more than ever. But race has been largely domesticated here, treated as an add-on element, an analogy or external metaphor, another intersectional axis to be managed, an ascriptive characteristic of the always already privileged human, rather than as a world-structuring system of meanings within which intrahuman and inter-species differences are consistently thought together. This has led to bracketing the suffering of racialized humans, disconnecting it from the suffering of nonhuman animals, and designating the latter alone as the paradigmatic victims most deserving of our ethical attention.

Racism as Zoological Witchcraft steps boldly and purposefully into this breach—not to build bridges or broker agreements but to question the very foundations of academic inquiry and political organizing around these issues. What many scholars and activists share, Ko argues, is an unfortunate tendency to conceptualize "racism," "speciesism," and other faces of oppression as discrete and separable issues. This reflects the lingering coloniality of their thinking, the way they inadvertently mimic the ideological scaffolding of power. (Intersectionality theorists, she warns, claim to resolve this problem by bringing categories into contact with each other, but they actually aggravate the problem by first doubling down on the reification of categories.) What we need to recognize, Ko argues, is that white supremacy is "multidimensional"—that is, it expresses itself through multiple registers, including "race" and "species," all of which are mutually constituted all the way down. Our current frameworks are not serving us well, then. Indeed, the architecture of resistance that we have built to challenge the social order has itself ossified into an order that must be exploded if we are to gain any meaningful traction against white supremacy. In this context, in Ko's view, nothing short of "a conceptual Big Bang" will do.

Ko's message to race scholars and activists is that they are trying in vain to hold the (question of the) animal at bay. It has already burrowed under the fence. It is already at the heart of their concerns. This is because white supremacy is zoological in character, and the concept of "animality" is the most important weapon in its arsenal. White supremacy is best understood as "zoological witchcraft," Ko argues—a pervasive, insatiable force seeking to consume, get inside of, and destroy those deemed to be "animal," namely, nonwhites and nonhumans. (Ko's use of this concept to analyze Jordan Peele's 2017 film *Get Out* is stunning and one of the highlights of the book.) Thus, race scholars and activists can no longer dismiss animality as an extraneous concern—they must overcome their anxious objections and face it head on. Deconstructing animality is not, as feared, a detour from racial liberation, but rather a crucial step along the path.

The takeaway for animal scholars and activists is perhaps more unsettling. Ko, a self-described vegan, asks whether a stand-alone animal movement is necessary or productive once racial activists are persuaded to embrace what she calls "afro-zoological resistance," or racial resistance that centers the question of the animal. If race and animality are not two discrete issues but mutually imbricated dimensions of white supremacy, doesn't the maintenance of two separate movements perpetuate confusion and hinder progress? That the (mainstream of the) contemporary animal movement is pervaded with capitalist logic—think of the "branding" of different movement organizations, the reduction of veganism to a "lifestyle choice," the conflation of consumerism with animal activism—only deepens Ko's skepticism about its long-term use value. Is the animal movement holding animals in captivity, she asks? Do animals need to be freed from it?

As a scholar trained in media studies, Ko self-consciously writes in the borderlands between popular culture and academia. *Racism as Zoological Witchcraft* is all about accessibility: the excellent illustrations and glossary of terms, as well as Ko's conversational writing style, indicate her commitment to communicating with the reader in simple, clear, straightforward language shorn of jargon and esoteric baggage. At the same time, Ko writes with unusual theoretical brilliance, citing and reflecting upon cutting-edge scholarship in philosophy, animal studies, feminist studies, history, and, especially, black studies. There is no forfeiture of sophistication for clarity—in other words, the reader gets a full measure of both. Having recognized, presciently, that there is a broad readership out there hungry for a deeper understanding of these matters, Ko opens up a new, hybrid space for thinking and talking about race and animality and invites us to join her in an ongoing conversation that is at once unnerving, exhilarating, and potentially liberatory. In 2019, in this moment of global racial crisis and ecological catastrophe, as settled modes of thinking persist despite their evident bankruptcy, we need more books like this one.

Claire Jean Kim
August 2019

NOTES BEFORE READING THIS GUIDE

1. Even though I touch upon subjects like animals and veganism, you do not need a particular dietary standard to engage with the concepts in this book. All too often, when I bring up topics relating to animals, people say, "But I'm not vegan." If someone who consumes meat publishes a book, do we assume that one is required to eat meat to read it? No. Similarly, you don't need a particular dietary standard to read about concepts relating to racism and animals. The goal of this book is to create a more accurate picture of what racism looks like, taking into account animal experiences.

2. Although I specifically write from the perspective of a mixed-race Black woman who is deeply interested in **decolonial** and critical race theory, and whereas I routinely use language like "we" and "ours" in reference to Black people more generally, this book is for anyone interested in liberatory futures for everyone. A particular racial identity isn't required to engage with the concepts in this book.

3. In 2017, I contributed an essay about animal liberation to the first *African American Vegan Starter Guide*, created by Tracye McQuirter. The guide helped Black folks learn about plant-based eating. However, this guide made me realize that there are no guides to help the public have accessible conversations about race and animals. I deliberately call this text a "guide" because I am offering tips on how to have conversations about racism and animality. I write in a very conversational style because I like to imagine having a face-to-face conversation with my readers. These topics can be pretty complex, and I want to break through that complexity by presenting these issues in a new and accessible way.

4. I use illustrations throughout this guide to bolster certain points I'm making. I merge illustrations with theory to support the larger theme of this book, which is to present ideas through new genres.

5. This book is not "intersectional." For some reason, any time a Black person talks about more than one oppression at a time, we are trained to think they're expressing this through an intersectional analysis, and I'm not. I will explore this further in the book.

6. I would urge you to watch Jordan Peele's 2017 movie *Get Out* before reading this book, considering my analysis contains many spoilers.

7. I would also urge you to check out the references at the back of the book for a comprehensive reading list about subjects relating to animality, race, consumption, decoloniality, and more.

8. Although I use the term *witchcraft* in the book to describe white supremacy's interactions with the oppressed (inspired by James Perkinson's scholarship), I am aware that witchcraft as a practice has many different iterations and frameworks. Additionally, witchcraft isn't necessarily "negative" or "destructive." A lot of people of color have reclaimed witchcraft as a practice for liberation.[1] In addition, a plethora of feminist scholarship interrogates the term *witch* in addition to reclaiming the term (Sollee 2017). I'm reminded of Yoko Ono's album *Yes, I'm a Witch*. Witchcraft has many different contexts and frameworks, and this book re-situates white ritualistic practices of oppression as a form of racial witchcraft practice itself, with specific reference to the ideas put forth by Perkinson.

9. In this book, I do not offer "practical" step-by-step solutions. Sometimes teaching people how to ask the right question *is* part of the solution.

Glossary of Terms

I bold the terms the first time they appear in the book to signal to readers that you can reference the glossary if you need to.

Afrofuturism: "Afrofuturism is often the umbrella for an amalgamation of narratives, but at its core, it values the power of creativity and imagination to reinvigorate culture and transcend social limitations. The resilience of the human spirit lies in our ability to imagine. The imagination is a tool of resistance" (Womack 2013, 24).

Afro-Zoological Resistance: A concept I created that centers on anti-racist activism that explicitly interrogates animality.

Animality: There are many different definitions of this concept; however, at its core, *animality* is a term that describes the social conditions of nonhuman animals. *Animality* also extends beyond literal nonhuman animal bodies and serves as a construction that cuts across race, gender, and class and reveals structures of power, anchored to the human. "[T]he emphasis in animality studies remains more on discursive constructions of animalities in relation to human cultural politics, rather than representations of nonhuman animals with more of an emphasis on improving the relationships and interactions between human and nonhuman animals" (Lundblad 2017, 11).

Decolonial: A theoretical framework that is interested in deconstructing/ undoing/de-linking Eurocentric ways of understanding the world. "Decoloniality is . . . the energy that does not allow the operation of the logic of coloniality nor believes the fairy tales of the rhetoric of modernity. . . . [Decolonial] thinking is . . . thinking that de-links and opens . . . to the possibilities hidden . . . by the modern rationality that is mounted and enclosed by categories of Greek, Latin, and the six modern imperial European languages" (Mignolo 2011).

Eurocentric: A worldview that privileges perspectives/theories/frameworks from Western/European culture.

Intersectionality: A concept created by legal scholar Kimberlé Crenshaw that states marginalized people sit at multiple intersections of oppression and can experience multiple types of oppression at one time. For example, Black women experience racism *and* sexism due to the intersections of oppression they sit at.

Minoritized: Rather than using the term *minority*, *minoritized* is a term that demonstrates the ways in which minorities are *actively* in the process of being marginalized. *Minoritized* is a verb, whereas *minority* is a noun. *Minoritized* puts the onus on the systems that harm those with less power (see Benitez 2010, 131).

Social Layerism: A term I coined in a 2016 talk titled "Afrofuturism and Black Veganism: Towards a New Citizenship" at the Intersectional Justice Conference at the Whidbey Institute. *Social layerism* refers to the ways in which intersectional activists and scholars often pile oppressions on top of one another without an "intersection" or "connection" ever really taking place.

Speciesism: A concept/theory that states animals are oppressed because they are not a part of the species *Homo sapiens*. *Speciesism* suggests humans are prejudiced toward other species because they believe themselves to be dominant and superior. *Speciesism* is often referred to as a system of oppression "like" racism or sexism.

Transmogrified: "The changing of something into a different form or appearance (especially a fantastic or grotesque one)" (Jackson 2016, 117).

Veganism: An ethical lifestyle devoted to not consuming animals in any capacity. There are many different sub-groups of vegans. Some are vegan for health reasons; others are vegan for ethical/political purposes and oppose animals being used in fashion, science experiments, and in entertainment.

White Supremacy: "By 'white supremacy' I do not mean to allude only to the self-conscious racism of white supremacist hate groups. I refer instead to a political, economic and cultural system in which whites overwhelmingly control power and material resources, conscious and unconscious ideas of white superiority and entitlement are widespread, and relations of white dominance and nonwhite subordination are daily reenacted across a broad array of institutions and social settings" (Ansley 1989, 1024).

Zoological Racism: A more descriptive term to capture the way that racism is maintained by the human/animal binary. Within this setup, white supremacy is both anti-Black and anti-animal.

Introduction

After I saw Jordan Peele's film *Get Out* in 2017, I remember leaving the theater feeling as if I were in a trance. As a theorist who regularly writes about anti-racism and animals, I was amazed at how well Peele wove together themes about anti-Blackness and **animality** in such a creative and deeply moving theatrical way. *Get Out*'s effect was similar to a slow-release tablet. Over time, the messages of the film started to reveal themselves to me and sparked a type of creativity that I, as a writer, had not felt in a long time.

Get Out succeeds so magnificently because it tackles large and complex theoretical subjects in a creative and imaginative way. It presents issues of racism and animality through a different genre; Peele shows us how we do not necessarily need to serve up stories about **white supremacy** through histories of slavery, or photographs of lynching, or traumatic modern-day narratives about police violence. We can use science fiction and comedy to highlight the uncomfortable layers to our experiences as racialized subjects.

Peele's film served as a creative wellspring for me when it came to thinking about how I wanted to present issues relating to animals and race to a public that has largely been trained by the media to view these two issues as perpetually in tension with each other. Writing theory about a particular cultural phenomenon like racism can be an incredibly exhausting experience. It sounds a bit funny, right? Some might wonder, "How can writing be exhausting?" However, trying to help others understand the deeper messages enveloped in a particular cultural norm can take every ounce of energy you have . . . especially when you try to present these issues in new and exciting ways. Brilliant theorists frequently present incredibly complex and profound ideas within the realm of academia, which is all too often isolated from popular media outlets. Over time, I have realized that the format and contextual references of a particular discussion, article, or literary work are just as important as the subjects being discussed.

As I continued to think about *Get Out* and all of the layered messages in the film, I stumbled across the scholarship of James Perkinson, an activist and professor of ethics and systematic theology. His work completely changed the trajectory of my own. In all honesty, without the combined psychological effect of *Get Out* and the scholarship of Perkinson, I would not have written this book. His essay "European Race Discourse as Witchcraft" (2004) and his book *Shamanism, Racism, and Hip-Hop Culture: Essays on White Supremacy and Black Subversion* (2005) presented issues of racism through a framework I had never encountered.

Perkinson constructs racism and years of colonial consuming as a modern-day **Eurocentric** witchcraft practice. At first, when I saw Eurocentric racism being called "witchcraft," it made me laugh: I wasn't accustomed to hearing something as normalized as white supremacy framed as a witchcraft practice. However, after I explored Perkinson's scholarship, I realized how his thinking is a cornerstone to understanding the inner workings of white supremacy. Like Peele, Perkinson presents a common issue (racism) in a completely genre-bending way. In particular, Perkinson examines the ways in which Christianity was historically used as a colonial tool to bolster white superiority. He writes:

> What [Jamaican-American philosopher Charles W.] Mills calls . . . "the Racial Contract," I am underscoring, out of its historical emergence, as a white witch pact. It creates an in-group of flesh consumers who share a secretive power/ knowledge designated . . . as "whiteness." It is, in fact . . . a form of "theological blackness" or witchery, rewritten as

ontology and anthropology. . . . It is the dissimulation of modern white supremacy, it is racial *discourse* itself that is the witchcraft *practice*. . . . (2004, 622)

After I read his work, I realized that Perkinson was creatively linking white supremacy to something beyond just a "system" or a "framework." White supremacy is so pervasive, and colonialism so consumptive and violent, that the word *system* does not seem to cover how expansive and conceptually penetrative it is. I think most of us, as members of the public, have become numb to the popular ways in which racism has been represented in the news and media. In part, this is due to the fact that we keep referring to white supremacy as just a "system" or "institution," rather than a living, insidious, expansive, colonial force that works to "get inside," consume, and destroy.

I started imagining how I could talk about controversial issues like anti-racism and animal rights through a new framework and a new genre altogether. In the past, I've felt I could only speak about these issues in animal rights and vegan spaces. I felt I could only package my message in ways that would be palatable for these movements, and this unfortunately forced me to trim parts of my message. It seems activists do that a lot in our movements: we edit our messages to ensure they "fit in" with dominant modes of thinking, and it's my belief this often prevents change from happening.

In 2017, I co-wrote my first book, *Aphro-ism: Essays on Pop Culture, Feminism, and Black Veganism from Two Sisters,* and I am expanding and building upon many of the concepts explored within that text.

◆

Throughout this book, I employ references to the notion of witchcraft, specifically in regard to Perkinson's work. However, I depart from it a bit because I include an analysis of animals that is often left out of discussions about colonial consumption. In this book, I do the following:

1. I use *witchcraft* as a metaphor to describe how white supremacy gets "inside" the oppressed and metabolizes their essences and souls.
2. I employ *witchcraft* as a metaphor to describe the current state of our social justice movements—spaces I believe are still controlled by Eurocentric thinking—as though we are all still in a racial trance, guided by colonial maps to create our liberation movements. And finally,
3. I draw upon Claire Jean Kim's work on **zoological racism** to demonstrate how white supremacy's witchcraft practice is zoological in nature and relies upon notions of the human and the animal to maintain its power and order.

I have realized through giving presentations and communicating with different audiences all over the United States that there is still some confusion around the relationship between animal oppression and racial oppression. In short, anti-racist activism is simply seen as Black Lives Matter and animal rights activism is largely seen as People for the Ethical Treatment of Animals, popularly known as PETA. These two spaces seem like they are perpetually in conflict with each other, and in this book I want to show a completely different way of broaching these topics that exists outside of the confines of modern-day mainstream liberation movements. I want you to think about the raw oppression itself—not the movements that have been created to tackle the oppression.

Whereas there are many scholars and academics writing robust theory about animals and race, much of that knowledge tends to stay in the halls of academia, or their thoughts stay sealed in academic journals that are largely inaccessible to the mainstream. In order to read these materials, you must either be enrolled in an academic institution, or you have to pay for access. When I left academia, my access to journals and articles was terminated, which prevented me from reading many of the cutting-edge ideas and arguments that were not available anywhere else. Luckily, the Internet allows a resourceful researcher other avenues for obtaining scholarly works (e.g. academia.edu, to name but one). Since a lot of cutting-edge arguments are difficult to find or even understand because of the academic language employed, I wanted to create an accessible book rooted in theory for audiences who crave a deeper understanding of these issues.

My academic background in media studies certainly informs the perspectives I present in this book. Media studies is a field that centers on the ways in which cultural artifacts such as movies, television, and books (i.e., media) communicate notions of power. My goal for this book is to use my training in these fields to create new toolkits for our activist efforts. Media studies is a fertile theoretical ground for activists to analyze contemporary power dynamics. Studying media can be difficult because they form a moving target—what is new becomes old very quickly. However, an incredible wealth of information is embedded in what might be considered "pop" media, particularly with regard to how our society constructs, interprets, and engages in social power dynamics in general. Although the landscape is always changing in the realm of media studies, it is no less deserving of analysis and attention.

Although it might be easy to dismiss media's influence, we can think of simple examples to demonstrate how certain media representations have shaped public discourse and have impacted our own moral systems. For example, we can think of Judge Judith Sheindlin, popularly known at Judge Judy, whose influence is oftentimes much more far-reaching and impactful than that of Supreme Court justices. In 2018, *The Hill* released an article that noted that more than half of the people in the United States couldn't name a single Supreme Court justice (Birnbaum 2018), whereas over 9.5 million people tune in daily to watch Judge Judy on television (Walsten 2017). Whether or not we agree with her comments, her lessons about morality and personal responsibility have left an impression on our culture: "Sheindlin's audience considers her a real-life kind of superhero: a no-nonsense, sassy arbiter of justice who punishes the guilty, scolds the swindlers, and defends the little guy. She does what we want the justice system to do" (Buckwalter 2014).

Because of her influence, Judge Judy is currently the highest-paid judge in the U.S. In 2018, she made over $47 million, whereas Supreme Court justices earn on average $255,000. The fact that Judge Judy makes more than Supreme Court justices demonstrates the value we see in her perspective on morality. Media become vehicles that scholars use to make sense of the world we live in as well as how our morals and values are shaped. That our current president, Donald Trump, is a reality-television star speaks to the undeniably important role television and film play in formulating our thoughts about ourselves as well as our notions about power. Although many disciplines, especially philosophy, Africana studies, and even gender studies, focus on animals and race, there has not yet been a strong critical media studies text that centers animality and race. I am trying to fill a gap in the literature by merging different theoretical frameworks while introducing new insights.

To be frank, though I call myself *vegan*, my work extends beyond the mainstream frameworks of **veganism**, which is regularly framed as just a diet or lifestyle. Despite the fact that I do not eat any animal products, I have wrestled for years with even calling myself *vegan*, because the label itself seems to instantaneously arrest people's imaginations regarding your activist potential. People immediately assume you are a chef or a hippie who is "privileged enough" to care about animals. Most members of the public associate veganism with food products, and I hope to disrupt this knee-jerk response.

I remember when I told friends and family that I was working on *Aphro-ism*, a book about Black vegan critical race theory, everyone asked if it was going to be a cookbook. That is how the mainstream narrative goes: *veganism is about food.* In fact, most of the objections to veganism are largely food-based as well. I'm sure you've noticed that most folks say that veganism isn't "accessible" to people who can't afford the foods, or a vegan diet is not possible for people with certain medical conditions. Many vegan activists already acknowledge this reality and are sensitive to the conditions in which **minoritized** people live, for whom access to vegan food is not always an option.[1] However, within these objections, veganism is still largely treated as a diet or a conversation strictly about consumption/food.

In fact, during the question-and-answer segment at the end of my lectures about animality and race, it has become commonplace for an audience member to ask a question such as "What about people who eat meat in [fill in the country]?" or for someone to enquire about "indigenous" communities. The question is usually framed as a "gotcha" moment to highlight moral inconsistences in veganism as a diet, which completely bypasses my theoretical offerings on animals and race.

For one, the behaviors that got us, as a species, to where we are should not necessarily be permissible from here onward. Additionally, my research and work do not center on an archeological analysis of how people have used animals throughout history. I am talking about animals within a very specific theoretical context. Even though I do not condone animal oppression, I am not going to retroactively moralize on people in the past, or people who are trying to survive today. Lastly, asking me about people who eat meat in another country bypasses the actual work that I do and furthermore re-centers food, rather than theory, as the topic of conversation. I am not in bioethics or archeology/anthropology; I am a racial theorist. There *are* scholars who do study indigenous communities and their relationships to animals (Runk 2019). Many people can't engage with topics relating to animals beyond food, and thus most of the questions I am asked center on the literal consumption of animal flesh.

However, food isn't just a quotidian "thing" that sits on our plates. Food should not be talked about as only a digestible item. As Breeze Harper notes:

> I simply cannot look at food as an "everyday mundane object." I understand the meanings applied to food as something that represents an entire culture's ideologies around everything. For example, food can tell me a society's expectations about sexuality, gender roles, racial hierarchies of power, and ability. (Nathman 2013)

I am constantly asked about literal food and literal animal bodies in part because the mainstream capitalist vegan/animal rights movement has equated veganism with kale or processed food products, rather than a critical intervention into race, power, animality, and thought. Although I understand that veganism *can* be about food, I am arguing that it shouldn't be about *only* or *strictly* food products. It is obviously not the job of a vegan sausage company to discuss the history of white supremacy and animality, so my commentary is not necessarily targeted at all members of the vegan community.

Because veganism has become so corporatized and chained to food items, it has become common for most people to dismiss it because it's been framed as a diet that's not affordable. Imagine if you heard someone say, "I can't be a Black Lives Matter activist because it costs too much!" or "Being a feminist is too expensive!" These statements are overtly absurd to those of us who understand that these movements are not about items or consumption, but powerful conversations for change.

My goal is not to shame people who cannot afford to eat a vegan diet. I am highlighting how veganism is *also* about powerful conversations. I understand that veganism relies upon a specific dietary standard; however, veganism can and should go beyond discourse about food or diet or identity. I would argue that I started to engage in vegan conceptual frameworks *long before*[2] I went vegan with regard to my diet. When we treat veganism as only a matter of what food one eats, it can feel as if we're holding the key to racial liberation in our hands but only conceive of it as a spoon.

In 2018, I was interviewed for *The New York Times* alongside other Black vegan activists. The article ran in the food section of the newspaper, which was disappointing considering "food" is not seen as a political issue in our mainstream collective consciousness. Placing a conversation about white supremacy and animality in the food section defangs the points being made in the article.[3] My hope is that one day these conversations will be moved into the race/politics section!

Shortly after the interview, a well-known website contacted me because they wanted to spotlight my work. Even though I was honored to receive such an invitation, I declined because the website wanted to write about my work in the lifestyle section of their magazine where they regularly featured stories on yoga and traveling. Filing my writing under the lifestyle section does not make much sense if you understand that I'm a theorist, not a health guru, nutritionist, or chef. Even on Facebook, someone posting about my work referred to me as a "Black vegan chef."

Many of the headline images people use in their blog posts to feature the theory I write include imagery of Black people holding vegetables or bags of food. When I am interviewed on podcasts or other digital publications, I am usually asked questions such as "Where can Black people in food deserts access fresh fruits and vegetables?" This is odd, considering I have never claimed to be a food-justice activist. Recently, I've even been getting interview requests to speak about Hip Hop and veganism, which baffles me because I don't believe I strike anyone as the type of person who is hip enough to even study this field! It is easy to collapse all Black vegan contributions into one box without understanding the nuances in our work. *I am a theorist*, and I hope this book further demonstrates that point.

Based on my experiences, I can safely say that there is a general air of confusion when it comes to understanding topics relating to race and animals, specifically when Black and Brown activists are articulating the concepts. On top of that, if you're Black and vegan, and you're not talking about environmental racism, food justice, diversity, or vegan soul food, most people do not necessarily know how to make sense of your activism.

If activists speak about communities of color that live near factory farms or those that do not have access to fresh foods, journalists understand this type of advocacy and attempt to spotlight it as much as they can. It *is* important and worthy of being highlighted. However, that is not the only sort of work people of color are capable of doing. When I say that I am a theorist who writes racial theory about animals and race, I am usually greeted with confused looks or blank stares. Thus, I have started to distance myself from some journalists who are eager to feature my work yet keep trying to place my interviews or essays in the obviously wrong sections of their website or magazine. Unfortunately, because most academic theory about race and animals is inaccessible to the mainstream, journalists have become "public intellectuals"; they frame these conversations for the public, and this has had detrimental consequences for our movements. Most (but not all) journalists I have encountered are after a "story" rather than trying to unpack theory for an audience.

Many writers categorize the world into neat sections on their website that fail to accommodate the multidimensionality of critical, decolonial analysis—sections such as lifestyle, politics, race, gender, and health, which you will find on many mainstream websites today. Journalists certainly did not create this setup. *Our entire society* is already filtered through clear-cut lenses that structure how we are trained to see and understand the world at large. We've reduced everything to the silos the dominant culture gave us.

As soon as we discover that someone is vegan, we immediately file their thoughts and words under the "meat-free," "health," or "PETA" argument. Most members of the public do not necessarily realize that veganism can be a movement about race, for example, or that vegan activists can engage with conversations about gender politics in very deep and complex ways like Carol Adams does in her book *The Sexual Politics of Meat*.

I've found that the separate pages that make up blogs and journalistic sites—such as lifestyle, race, gender, politics, etc.—represent but one component of the media landscape that provides overt and covert suggestions about how we should conceive of our social worlds. We need to re-evaluate how much we rely upon these social filing cabinets in our activist movements. Classification as a general tool for organization isn't necessarily destructive; however, social categories that have been born out of a toxic historical and geopolitical structure can prevent us from understanding the full picture of a particular concept. In fact, I feel this is exactly what they have been designed to do.

Truthfully, we as activists already know how limiting these social categories that organize how we see the world can be. We can think of the fatigue a lot of activists feel at the tragic news of a white male shooting up a school or an event space, followed by the conversation predictably turning to "mental health"[4] or "gun control." Activists have already expressed countless times that if a Brown or Black man committed the same violent act, this would immediately be considered an act of terrorism (Butler 2015).

Mainstream news coverage tends to configure its understanding of a violent act based on the perpetrator's body. As soon as we see which body has done the violence, we know which cabinet to file that violence in, which prevents us from finding viable solutions to the problem. For example, when Nikolas Cruz murdered 17 students in Parkland, Florida, on February 14, 2018, predictably mental health and gun control were the topics of conversation. However, by examining his acts only through those lenses, we miss that Cruz had a history of domestic violence (Haldevang 2018), and harbored incredibly racist thoughts and attitudes toward minoritized groups (Obeidallah 2018). When white men commit violent acts, we tend to individualize their behaviors and hyper-analyze specific episodes in their lives that contributed to their "mental health" problem, rather than looking at them as a group. We tend to reserve "groupthinking" for people of color.

Many activists already understand how destructive it is to organize our understanding of violence based solely on the perpetrator's looks. However, we replicate this error in our *liberation movements*, which similarly lack an honest and nuanced analysis. As soon as we see which body is being *violated*, we file their experience of injustice in a specific conceptual filing cabinet, which forces us to think about their liberation through a specific limiting filter.

For example, when animals are harmed, we feel an urge to respond with an "animal rights toolkit"—we discuss **speciesism**, factory farming, and veganism. When Black people are harmed, we have an "anti-racist toolkit" at our disposal that discusses police violence and Black Lives Matter. When women are violated, we have a "feminist toolkit" discussing **intersectionality** and gender-based violence. The list goes on and on. We have separate filing cabinets for each violated body, and within those filing cabinets we have folders that contain literature describing how one should think about and envision solutions to the problem.

However, I am arguing that this arrangement *itself* is the problem. Looking at a victim's body and having a reflex that guides how we should immediately perceive the problem and the solution, we are already missing certain dimensions of the violation, and are thus limited in our tools to create adequate solutions. Our categorical thinking prevents us from thinking outside the box. Many activists have a sense that something is wrong or limiting about our categorical activist setup, especially when it comes to wanting to fight for multiple violated bodies at *one time*. Most people of color who advocate animal rights and anti-racism tend to face social obstacles in their pursuits. We are often interrogated about our commitment to anti-racism since we are simultaneously invested in the fight to liberate animals.

Women of color in general face a similar constraint when it comes to the feminist and anti-racist movements. Women of color know they experience racist as well as sexist oppression; however, should we join the anti-racist movement or the feminist movement? Will joining both really cure the invisibility we feel? Rather than abandoning both movements and creating something new, well-intentioned activists (especially activists of color) have been assuming that intersectionality is a relief from these categorical constraints. Intersectionality posits that multiple systems of oppression *can* intersect, which means different groups of minoritized people can experience multiple oppressions simultaneously. For example, if you are a woman of color who is disabled, one would say that you sit at multiple intersections of oppression and you experience racialized sexism and ableism.[5]

However, I argue that intersectionality isn't a resistance to or relief from colonized categorical thinking, but reaffirms it. Although activists are accustomed to taking "race," "gender," and "class" and making them intersect, most people don't question how they have been trained to understand what "race," "gender," and "class" are to begin with. The reason why Black women are excluded from both the anti-racist movement and the feminist movement is because our cultural understandings of what constitutes a "Black person" and what constitutes a "woman" are already tainted and separated at the root.

The mainstream public thinks of a "Black person" as a man and a "woman" as a white female. Making these two spaces connect doesn't discursively birth a Black woman. Activists take these terms and start building conceptual architecture with it; in my work, I like to question how we have come to understand these terms. As philosopher Maria Lugones writes, "If woman and Black are terms for homogenous, atomic, separable categories, then their intersection shows us the absence of Black women rather than their presence. So to see non-white women is to exceed 'categorical' logic" (2010, 742).

Intersectionality is more like one highway crossing over another highway. From an aerial view, this could look like two roads intersecting, but they are actually two separate and distinct roads with two different heights, and in between them is a gap—a void.

It's an illusion of an intersection at a distance, however. When you close the distance and start to approach this supposed intersection, you immediately see the roads are not even touching. This is in part why we struggle with making Black women visible within intersectional spaces (where we merge the "race" road and the "gender" road) . . . they live within the gaps: "When one is trying to understand women at the intersection of race, class, and gender, non-white Black, mestizo, indigenous, and Asian women are impossible beings" (Lugones 2010, 757).

For true liberation, I do not encourage intersectional or interdisciplinary thinking; I encourage "un-disciplinary" thinking.[6] *The only way forward is to transcend disciplinary logic.* The disciplines themselves (race, gender, class, etc.) are already infected with coloniality. The social categories were born out of an oppressive system—the very system activists are claiming to fight. Making colonized social categories "intersect" doesn't rid the structure of coloniality and it bypasses the work we need to do within the categories themselves.[7]

I argue that what Black women in particular are experiencing isn't an *intersection* of sexism and racism, which has popularly been called *misogynoir.*[8] There has to be an entirely different setup to talk about our experiences; this requires us to undo these "intersections" and dissect the actual categories themselves to re-shape and re-mold them. In this book, I go into further detail to explain why I believe intersectionality isn't the best framework to analyze multidimensional oppressions. We need to advocate epistemic ruptures in the current ways in which we understand the world and how to solve its problems.

What I advocate in my work is akin to a conceptual Big Bang. If we understand the Big Bang in an astronomical context to be the cosmological event that sparked an entire new universe that, over time, became filled with galaxies and solar systems, then we need new universes of thought and new galaxies of theory in our social movements. We need to change the way that we think about the world and its inhabitants in order to create liberation movements that can effect change. Our current liberation movements are part of the problem of oppression!

Racism as Zoological Witchcraft is a project similar to those of many other creative and analytical thinkers who fight the disciplinary arrangement of knowledge: I want to engage in a process of undisciplining the ways in which activists filter oppression and liberation. I want us to think outside the box and re-examine the oppressions we see before us, all the while taking our time to re-learn how we should think about oppression and liberation.

Throughout this book, I refer to the animal rights movement and the anti-racist movement, particularly because there is so much tension around these two subjects. However, my analysis can be applied to other social justice movements as well. I examine the animal rights and anti-racist movements because there is so much material to work with. Nonetheless, I must note that despite the fact that I regularly interrogate animal rights and anti-racist spaces, I care about many other social justice issues as well. As I once stated in an interview: "As an activist, I always gravitate towards issues that are the most sensitive or controversial. I love focusing on the 'sore spots,' you know, the issues that spark the most emotion and tension, because within that tension we are often clinging to coloniality in some way" (VILDA team 2019).

The animal rights and anti-racist movements exist in tension in part because we are analyzing these two oppressions without having access to all of the theoretical tools we need. Therefore, I argue that the tension shouldn't be between animal rights and Black rights (as the media like to portray it) but in the theory and frameworks we have been forced to adopt in our social justice movements to explain why oppressive behavior happens to begin with. We cannot properly get out of this ideological mess if we don't take the time to figure out what went wrong in these movements.

This theoretical mess signals that a much larger issue exists: *All of the contemporary liberation movements in the U.S. are operating through colonial logic.* Therefore, this book isn't just about educating you on race and animals, but it's pointing to a larger call to action, which can be summarized as follows:

> We need to be as critical of our liberation movements as we are of the oppressive systems because they mirror one another. Our understanding of the world, our understanding of social categories, and our understanding of ourselves have been birthed from a toxic, oppressive, colonized cultural womb. If you're committed to fighting oppression, you might want to start in your activist spaces.

In this book, I argue that if we want to "get out" of this oppressive setup, we have to properly understand how we got in.

Here is an outline of each chapter of *Racism as Zoological Witchcraft.*

Chapter I explores popular media to explain the disconnect between anti-racist activism and animal rights activism. This requires me to unpack how the public and the media engage with these topics and present these issues. I offer alternative explanations for why I believe the tensions exist.

Chapter 2 analyzes examples from television and film, in particular *Get Out*, to demonstrate how animal corpses become emblems of white supremacy and how white supremacy's grammar system is consumption. In particular, I analyze taxidermy and introduce a new term to discuss white supremacy's ability to "get inside" the oppressed and re-define us. I examine racism as a form of zoological witchcraft that metabolizes bodies and essences and re-defines the experience of being oppressed.

Chapter 3 expands upon multidimensional liberation theory to demonstrate the deep relationships between systems of oppression. To accomplish this, I offer a critique of intersectionality. I argue that systems of oppression are more than just "connected"—they are composed of one another.

Chapter 4 revisits *Get Out* to show how **afro-zoological resistance** is the new frontier of multidimensional activism, and in Chapter 5, I discuss why the animal rights movement might not be the best political space to free animals.

Overall, I look at the ways in which racism functions like a zoological witchcraft practice and how part of its sorcery is found in our grasp of conceptual structures and in liberation movements that actually work to strengthen the system.

Lastly, I want to note that I am running with the assumption that you agree that animals are in a dire situation. I am not trying to convince anyone that such a plight exists. Whereas other authors do spend time convincing their readers that the horrid conditions of factory farms, for example, are cruel and unethical, this book analyzes segments of our collective psychology that rhetorically reinforce and naturalize such horrid treatment of animals, while also shining a light on the elusive interplay between race and the notion of animality.

1

Anti-Racism
vs.
Animal Liberation

*Popular Explanations for the Tension
Between Black Rights and Animal Rights*

Im'ma wear fur every day until they stop killing Black people.
When the police stop killing Black people, I'll stop wearing
fur. It's my new protest. So sorry, PETA! Don't be mad at me.
Be mad at the police. When they stop killing Black people,
I'll stop wearing fur. . . .—**Tiffany Haddish** (Dorsey 2018)

Why are we bringing race into this?—**Facebook comment**
from an animal rights activist

IF YOU WERE TO EXAMINE ONLY THE NEWS OR SOCIAL MEDIA WEBSITES TO understand why Black liberation groups currently exist in tension with animal rights groups, you would probably encounter one of the following reasons. Although this list certainly is not exhaustive, these are the most dominant reasons I have seen online:

a) Black people are trying to attain human rights for themselves, and asking them to morally consider animals (who are often unquestionably seen as disposable) is offensive.

b) Animal rights groups have produced insensitive, racist campaigns that have borrowed the history of Black struggles such as slavery and lynching to bring about sympathy for animals, without simultaneously fighting for Black rights.

c) White vegans, more generally, have created an inhospitable environment for people of color, and in turn, people of color feel as though veganism and animal rights aren't spaces for them.

In this chapter, I analyze these explanations as well as offer alternative reasons for why I believe the tension between the two groups exists. I also offer different ways in which we might think about the entanglements between race and animal oppression to move the conversation forward.

It's no secret that Black people in particular have a complicated relationship with animals today, due to white colonial expansions and their aftermath. The history of racial terrorism in the U.S. and around the world has perpetuated the idea that Black people are in some way more animal than human. That history has often resulted in people of African descent, especially in the U.S., distancing themselves from animals and their plight. I would argue that most Black people and people of color in the U.S. know that being associated with animals is cause for our own disposability.

This notion has all too often been reinforced: from law enforcement officers referring to Black people as "apes" and "monkeys" (Egelko 2018) to President Donald Trump calling a former Black staff member a "dog" (Shear 2018). In 2018, after the popular fashion brand H&M released an advertisement featuring a Black boy wearing a shirt with the text "The Coolest Monkey in the Jungle," people of African descent all over the world erupted in protest. Many Black people vowed to stop buying H&M products, and in at least one instance, an H&M store was vandalized (Politi 2018). This example alone illustrates that being associated with animals is considered by most Black people to be a profound insult.

Even in the vegan landscape, I have observed that many vegans of color don't mind bringing up health, food deserts, and food justice. However, when it comes to talking about the plight of actual nonhuman animals, there *can* be immediate discomfort and rejection.[1] I can't tell you how many conferences and vegfests I've been to where a majority of the Black speakers touched upon every subject relating to health and food but completely talked *around* animals and animality.

I'm reminded of a meeting I attended of Black vegans who wanted to create a conference. One participant stated: "We need to center health and wellness . . . we can't focus on animals though, because Black folks don't vibe with that message." The logic goes something like this: Because Black people are dealing with being animalized in society, and because we still need to work on securing rights for ourselves, it's inappropriate to tell us to start caring about animals as well. Health and wellness conversations often have absolutely nothing to do with animals. Yet, because the foods that are being advertised in wellness spaces *happen* to be plant-based (meaning they don't usually contain any animal products), such conversations are framed as being in the same landscape as animal rights. I argue that these are merely adjacent: they touch, but they are not necessarily in conversation with one another.[2]

On Instagram, someone once responded to my scholarship on race and animals through the comment below (the Instagram post is in its original form):

Why can't black ppl just for once focus on their own issues?!
You don't see any other ethnic group (Jews, Arabs, etc.) focus
on other stuff/groups except for black ppl. Some black ppl
were willing to protest against the "Muslim ban" but weren't
willing to march for Phillnado Castile. Now you have some
folks putting animal rights before black issues. Smh. How
about, just for once, we put RACE first. Love animals, but I
can't support animal rights while my brothers and sisters are
getting killed in cold blood everyday. Black ppl have already
enough on their plate. Let Becky and Chandler deal with
animal rights.

I see different iterations of this sentiment expressed all over the Internet
by well-intentioned anti-racist activists who associate a concern for
animals with a direct *lack* of concern for Black rights. The Instagram
comment is a prime example of how conversations about animal rights
and Blackness usually unfold in the public sphere. I think perhaps two
archetypal questions have emerged:

a) Why is it that Black folks are willing to show up and organize
for other oppressions but forget to address their own?
b) Why is it that white people are willing to risk their lives for
animals but regularly disregard the disposability of Black lives?

Unfortunately, these two questions have served as conversational
roadblocks in most discussions about race and animals. I've found that
urging Black people to re-think the relationships between animals and race
is framed as a racial insensitivity *in and of itself*. In fact, I have observed that
in the news and on social media, *advocating animal rights is oftentimes portrayed
as anti-Black—as anti-Black as police violence itself.* This is perhaps why a lot of
anti-racist activists specifically reference police brutality—exemplified
by the above Instagrammer's mention of Philando Castile, who was shot

and killed by a police officer in 2016—to bypass conversations about institutionalized animal suffering.

We can think of popular African American actress and comedian Tiffany Haddish, who in early 2019 recorded a video in which she stated, "I will continue to wear fur every single day until police stop killing Black people." She is not the only person who has made an argument like this. After Cecil the Lion was gunned down in 2015, the Huffington Post released an article stating:

> It seems like Americans, in general, found it easier to condemn a man who killed a lion than to criticize police officers who abuse their power. It took more than six months to simply bring charges against the Cleveland officer who killed Tamir Rice, an unarmed, 12-year-old child who was shot to death while playing at a park. It took over a year for an off-duty Chicago cop to be charged for Rekia Boyd's death. (Craven & Bellware 2015)

I am so accustomed to reading comments like this that I often forget that they don't really reflect the current reality of the landscape. It's easy to prove that most people in the U.S. are outraged by the unjust killing of Black people at the hands of police officers, if we look at the massive amount of media attention and support Black Lives Matter receives. Alicia Garza, one of the founders of Black Lives Matter, was actually invited by then-president Barack Obama to attend the State of the Union Address in 2016. Although celebrities like Jimmy Kimmel, for example, do publicly *express* concern for specific animals (like Cecil), it is important to note that many of those same celebrities regularly consume animal bodies, so their allegiance to animal liberation is questionable.

Due to the fact that many contemporary anti-racist activists are not familiar with scholarship that *links* animal oppression *to* racism, they cling to acts of, say, white-on-Black police violence to prove to the public that racism still exists. They purposely hyper-represent this form of violence because a) it is physical and observable and b) there is an obvious culprit—a white person. In our cultural setup, marginalized folks often operate as though only one "group" can acquire liberation at a time. I often imagine one microphone on a stage with a long line of minoritized groups waiting to get a chance to get the spotlight to speak to the audience composed of predominantly white people. This means that if any other group gets the spotlight, it is seen as directly taking time away from other groups and their causes.

By virtue of having to fight for power *amongst* nonhuman animal bodies in a white supremacist environment, anti-racist activists should recognize that animals might have something deeper to do with the conversation about race. Unfortunately, the reality is that people are dealing with real oppression, and our movements often encourage us to examine only our own oppression—in isolation from others.

Sometimes, when you're marginalized, it can feel like you're forced to wear a backpack with a lot of weight. I remember, as an undergraduate, reading an article by Peggy McIntosh (1988) in which she lists the different privileges that white people experience and that they discursively carry around every day. The article is popularly referred to as the "Knapsack of Invisible Privileges." However, I never understood why McIntosh used a backpack as metaphor, which suggests someone is carrying weight. I do not believe that privilege is a burden, so I'm going to adopt McIntosh's metaphor and call it a "Knapsack of Oppression." I'm sure there have been many iterations of this knapsack of oppression, so I am not claiming that I invented the idea. This knapsack contains the oppressive things some of us carry around from day to day, whether it's racism, trans-antagonism, poverty, or ableism. It's important to note that though the metaphor of a knapsack suggests one can "take off" the weight, for the purposes of this analogy we will imagine that people are unable to do this.

When animal rights activists (of all races) come along and start telling anti-racist activists to also start caring about animals, it can feel as though they want to add an extra burden to the weight people of color are already walking around with every day. The *current* way that animal rights activists and vegans typically try to get people of color involved in animal rights is often inappropriate (I've been guilty of this myself). I say this because as activists, we are borrowing Eurocentric ways of talking about animal oppression that completely ignore effective alternatives that don't rely upon comparisons or nebulous narratives anchored to "compassion."

People of color's experiences with animalization can and should be a fertile starting point and bridge for discussing animality and animal oppression. But it certainly does not mean that one should appeal to "comparisons" between animal oppression and Black oppression, as many vegans have tried to do, to accomplish this. *The goal should center on getting anti-racist movements to talk about animality, rather than trying to create strategies to get people of color to join the dominant animal rights movement.* Additionally, the emphasis on trying to get people of color to go vegan completely misses the mark in terms of what our goals should be, and I explain why that is the case throughout this book.

Frankly, this is where animal activists become poor representatives of the issues they care about the most. Animal activists regurgitate the same points about compassion and factory farming without having a larger intellectual framework or theoretical analysis. I have found that many authors and theorists who have no affiliation with major animal rights organizations make better and more compelling arguments on behalf of animals than traditional animal rights activists.

Lindgren Johnson (2018) puts forth a similar idea when she discusses the "*in*direct ways that African Americans become involved, in the midst of the fight for racial justice, in fundamental and deeply ethical questions surrounding animals and animality that exceed the limits of traditional animal activist and human rights discourses. . . . This 'indirect' engagement reflects their position as animal agents rather than mere animal advocates . . . " (20).

In trying to get Black and Brown people to join the dominant animal rights organizations, animal rights activists often fail to see how anti-racist movements already have fertile ground to interrogate animal oppression (often in more complex and dynamic ways). Most social justice movements today have become "brands" or spaces dominated by nonprofits and for-profit organizations. This corporatization may have the unfortunate effect of shifting the goal from getting people to understand the issues to getting people to join a particular group, brand, or identity. Again, I think it would be safe to say that most of the public equates animal rights with PETA. If one does not vibe with PETA as an organization, the assumption is that that person doesn't vibe with animal rights more broadly, which is a problem. The goal of *my* activism is in part to help minoritized folks understand that they are *already partici-pating* in the animal conversation by acknowledging that white supremacy treats them "like animals." My goal here is to help further develop that racial sensibility.

Racial activism does not exist in opposition to the goals of the animal rights movement; the two just operate from two different vantage points. Racial activists (like me) who include animals in their analyses acknowledge that this idea of "race" has oppressed humans and animals, and typically animal rights activists focus solely on "speciesism" as the dominant mode of animal oppression. Honestly, I used to be an activist who described herself as "anti-speciesist" until I started reading more decolonial scholarship on race and animals.[3]

Organizing animal experiences around "speciesism" is not neces-sarily flawed; it just offers an incomplete picture of what the problem is. Telling people of color to overtly or covertly push aside their experi-ences with animality to fight for animals is like trying to diagnose a medical issue in a body without taking a holistic look at the underlying condition. In order to have an accurate conceptual diagnosis and cure for animal oppression, we cannot focus on just the obvious symptoms, because we could easily mistake the symptoms for a different concep-tual disease.

To further draw upon the analogy, most of us have experienced the frustration of doctors who have been medically trained to specialize in only one part of the body. Imagine that a rash appears on your face one day; naturally, one would assume that you should make an appoint-ment with a dermatologist, who is trained to study the skin. Based on the tools and knowledge the dermatologist has, they might see only an allergy and prescribe a topical cream to heal the inflammation. However, if you go to a holistic doctor, they might start asking about your diet and reveal that you might have a gastrointestinal problem that can cause skin issues. Rather than prescribing a cream, your doctor might tell you to take probiotics, eat a plant-based diet, and add fermented foods to your plate. In other words, sometimes the obvious symptoms have a deeper root. Both doctors are invested in the same goal: to get rid of your rash. However, they have two very different approaches due to their different knowledge bases.

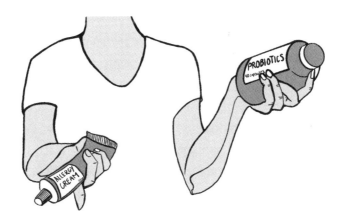

Similarly, holistic social theory can examine oppression from multiple angles. When we examine animal oppression, we need to look at factors other than just the obvious or surface-level symptoms, such as factory farming or speciesism. Factory farming is not the cause but the *result* of something else horrible that's occurring. Black and Brown activists may have a different conceptual diagnosis for the issue based on our own experiences with the dominant system, which can only bring more solutions to the table. Black experiences with zoological racism (racism anchored to the human/animal binary) should not be treated as an inconvenience to animal rights theory; it should be used to bolster our understanding of both what "animal" means and how the category of *Homo sapiens* does not necessarily provide refuge from zoological terrorism.

Unfortunately, though, because of the urgency of getting people involved in animal rights spaces due to the grotesque nature of animal abuse, our movements tend to rush and sloppily try to make *veganism* appeal to Black folks. Even though I am personally a proponent of veganism and I run my own website called Black Vegans Rock,[4] I do not subscribe to the idea that veganism should be used as the dominant vehicle to discuss *all* animal experiences. Activists take terms and start applying those terms to all actions they perceive as being aligned with their cause. If someone has a project that interrogates animality and race, vegan activists immediately label that work *vegan*.

The label *vegan* has a particular historical legacy anchored to speciesism theory. Not all activists and thinkers who write about animals are using speciesism as a framework or are discussing the literal consumption of nonhuman animal bodies. Rather than trying to smuggle all of these complex conversations about animals under the *vegan* label, we should get to a point in our activism where we recognize that conversations about race and animality often exceed the boundaries of vegan discourse, and that this should be celebrated rather than appropriated.

I see this same phenomenon happening in feminist spaces as well. Feminists try to re-frame all of women's actions (that are perceived as empowering) as *feminist* without realizing that feminism has a particular historical legacy anchored to white women's efforts to secure the vote and rights equal to those held by white men.[5] Trying to re-frame all of women's global efforts for freedom (in the past and present) as "feminist" is both ahistorical and inaccurate.

In using only mainstream veganism as the vehicle to talk about animals, we also miss out on the point that Black folks shouldn't contribute to animal suffering not only because the animal agriculture system is cruel and violent, but also because it is specifically anti-Black in this current cultural setup! Sincere Kirabo (2017) wrote an article about my views on anti-racism and animals and accurately pointed out that the liberation I envision is "less about meat consumption and more about the necessity of re-framing racism to include the relationship between anti-Blackness and anti-animal sentiment as codified into the white supremacist capitalist patriarchy. It is this cultural arrangement that informs our overall conceptualization of, and justifications for, meat consumption in white supremacist capitalist patriarchal societies."

The push to package all discourse concerning animals under the *vegan* label bypasses important conversations about racism and animality that need to take place. It also suggests that getting someone to eat a vegan diet means that you are simultaneously getting that person to morally consider animals, which is not necessarily true. I have found that this term *vegan* has been intellectually destructive to a lot of the theoretical work I do on animals and race. There needs to be a more robust understanding of racism that includes examining the notion of race through a zoological framework.

This is the primary difference between my work and that of the mainstream animal rights movement. I'm not interested in being just "anti-speciesist." I am interested in looking at how the socio-historical conception of the animal informs our notion of racism itself. I feel this is the best path toward freeing Black folks from the system of white supremacy while simultaneously tackling animal oppression. I also recognize that other avenues might emerge over time. Like other decolonial activists and thinkers, I am interested in building a more multidimensional and robust picture of what racism looks like, including an interrogation of the structures that harm animals.

As you move through this book, please keep in mind that when I discuss animal oppression, my goal isn't to add extra weight to the back-pack of oppression you are forced to carry every day, nor am I asking you to have a *basic* engagement with mainstream veganism. My goal is to show you how animality (a construct that oppresses anyone who deviates from what our culture considers to be an ideal human) is an integral part of all of the oppression *you are already experiencing each day.*

All I'm asking of you, as a Black or Brown person struggling in this system, is to re-introduce yourself to the oppressions you are already carrying because there are dimensions within them that already accommodate the ideas I am writing about. As people of color, we won't reach racial liberation by examining only the violence we experience, in isolation from other current social phenomena. We need to understand that this narrative of animality is the *real problem* and that in order to meaningfully liberate animals and ourselves, we have to deal with and attack it. This is why people of color and their unique experiences in this system matter in relation to animals. This work may be a bit disorienting at first because it's new, and perhaps what I am presenting here has a different flavor from the activism we're accustomed to seeing depicted in the news and on television.

In thinking about comments from minoritized people who tell me to "put race first" when I start to discuss animals, I want to demonstrate how including animals in our racial analyses isn't a distraction from racism; it is crucial to understanding racism's fabric.

White Supremacy as a Zoological Machine

I've already discussed the *tensions* between Black liberation groups and animal rights groups. Now I want to discuss the *entanglements* between racial oppression and animal oppression on a theoretical level. If we want people to understand these entanglements, we have to look beyond the existent movements and examine the actual oppressions themselves to guide our activism. I would encourage others to distinguish the raw components of actual oppressions without a particular popular movement telling us how we should think about them.

When you are an animal or are subhuman, your degradation is justified:

> What does it mean to be a nonhuman? As a nonhuman, your life is not valued. You are an "alien," "foreign," "exotic," "savage"—a wild one to be conquered or a nuisance to be destroyed. Your bodies are not your own, fit for probing and research. You have no history of value. You are incapable of creating culture in general, but when you do, it is from an impulse or emotion, never intellect. Humans, well-meaning or otherwise, can't relate to a nonhuman. (Womack 2013, 32–3)

Another marker of being animalized that we often leave out of the discussion is the ability to be consumed, both literally and figuratively. In *The Delectable Negro: Human Consumption and Homoeroticism within US Slave Culture* (2014), Vincent Woodard writes: "In slave narratives and ex-slave interviews, black persons correlated white consumptive appetites with southern codes of honor and nobility" (62). People of color know that our culture often frames us as more animal than human . . . in fact, Black people draw upon this legacy when fighting for our human rights. I can't tell you how many times I have heard anti-racist activists say things like "We are human" or "Stop treating us like animals!" when fighting white supremacist violence. Despite the fact that we belong to the species *Homo sapiens,* we know our oppression is anchored to our assignment as "subhuman" in this particular cultural setup.

Just as racial oppression is anchored to animality, animal oppression is anchored to race. Now, in order to understand how "animal" is a racial construct, we need to expand our understanding of white supremacy. I'm not saying that we need to add to our definitions of white supremacy; I'm saying that the movements we've been filtering our understanding of oppression through have not shown us the full landscape of what white supremacy actually looks like. It's almost like you've only been given ten pieces of a twenty-piece jigsaw puzzle, and you've been inaccurately told that the gaps are a natural part of the image.

As I've stated previously, "You can't create effective liberation movements if you don't completely understand the anatomy of your oppression" (Ko & Ko 2017, 94). Today, a lot of people struggle with understanding how expansive white supremacy is. Racism isn't just about skin tone . . . it's also about animality. When I give presentations or participate in interviews, a standard question I am routinely asked is "Why are you bringing animals into conversations about race?!" My response is: *I didn't bring animals into race . . . white supremacy did.* As the image below shows, this hierarchy was used by Josiah Nott to classify the natural world and demonstrate the superiority of whites and the inferiority of everyone else.

There are countless other types of historical images that capture the antiquated classification systems aimed at categorizing human appearance and behavior (Kim 2015). However, the one on the next page does a great job of illustrating the main point: that white supremacy relies upon zoological ideas to bolster its power.

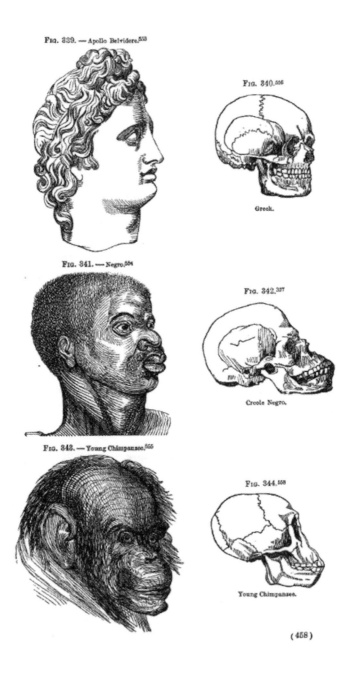

Figure I. (Figures 339–344 in Nott and Gliddon's [1854]

Types of Mankind or Ethnological Researches, p. 458)

That the system of white supremacy included animals in its racial hierarchy wasn't accidental. There is no way that we can get around talking about animals. No racial liberation movement will ever be successful without grappling with the situation of the animal. So when people tell me that people of color just need to "put race first" or just "focus on racism," I let them know that they have a narrow definition of racism because technically, by talking about animals and how we perceive and categorize them, I *am* talking about the system of race. What animals are experiencing *should* matter to our anti-racist movements if we understand that "animal" as a social construct was designed to prop up the ruling class and the "human." Although pre-colonial cultures all over the world consumed animal flesh, colonization added a racial connotation to "animal" and used this as a justification to brutalize different beings globally.

Animal doesn't just mean "cat" or "squirrel" or "cow." *Animal* is a label. It's a social construct the dominant class created to mark certain bodies as disposable without even a second thought. *Animal* as a term does not exist on its own . . . it's relational. It only makes sense in relation to the white human. Those who deem themselves the superior humans decide who falls within the category of *animal* by using their own group's traits as the standard measurement. *Animal* is a signifier that is always convenient and changing, and any group the dominant class deems unworthy is immediately branded with this label.

Imagine you have a glass you always drink out of. One day you might put coffee in it; the next you might pour in some orange juice. Despite the fact that the types of liquid in the glass might change, the glass's function does not. Juice and coffee as liquids don't have much in common (besides being water-based) except that they are forced to take on the shape of the glass.

That's how the term *animal* operates: as a label it captures how the compulsory elimination and consumption of certain bodies, as well as the bodies shoved under "animal," have the capacity to change with time. Black people and animals have been purposely molded into certain shapes by the oppressive system (the glass) to fit the contours of its needs: "Arguably, plasticization is the fundamental violation of enslavement: not any one particular form of violence . . . but rather coerced formlessness as a mode of domination" (Jackson 2016, 118).

Claire Jean Kim (2017) writes: "Blackness and animalness, then, form poles in a closed loop of meaning. Blackness is a species construct (meaning 'in proximity to the animal') and animalness is a racial construct (meaning 'in proximity to the black'), and the two are dynamically interconstituted all the way down. In this sense, the anti-Black social order that props up the 'human' is also a zoological order, or what we might call a zoologo-racial order" (10).

So, what Black folks are experiencing is a type of animality and what animals are experiencing is a type of racialization. This means that the *current ways* in which we've been discussing racism and animal oppression do not accommodate a more complex understanding of what's really happening. We cannot possibly create effective liberation movements if we don't understand how these phenomena are intrinsically entangled and how they constitute one another. The zoologo-racial order is the true foundation of white supremacy.

In the next chapter, I examine this zoologo-racial construction even further and detail how white supremacy functions as a form of zoological witchcraft, metabolizing the souls and essences of the oppressed. The next chapter demonstrates how entangled these subjects are, and how they reach beyond simple conversations about veganism into a different terrain: understanding the scope and size of racism by examining the treatment of animals and racialized subjects in contemporary life.

2

WHITE SUPREMACY
AS
ZOOLOGICAL WITCHCRAFT

Mediated Representations
of White Supremacy's Zoological Racism

Whiteness is a fantasy-scape; blackness is deep night. White is fascinated with devouring. Black is a gnawed bone of terror. Whiteness is the unconsciously cannibalistic predilection to eat "God"; blackness is the post-traumatic stress syndrome of being eaten by "God." Which "which" is really witch?
—**James W. Perkinson** (2004, 627)

[T]he "human" is paradigmatically both not-animal and not-black, birthed through the simultaneous application of these two caesurae, requiring the presence of both the "animal" and the "black" to locate itself.—**Claire Jean Kim** (2016, 45)

IN THIS CHAPTER, I AM GOING TO ATTEMPT TO ILLUMINATE A DIFFERENT way of approaching the animal conversation, using race as a vehicle. I also want to demonstrate how the literal consumption of nonhuman bodies is preceded by metaphorical consumption. This can be another direction to point people in when you want them to morally consider animals within this particular cultural setup.

In the following chapters, I analyze a couple of television shows and a film whose storylines deal with race. After giving talks all over the U.S. about race and animals, I have found that media examples tend to be the most successful at illustrating complex theory because they provide the audience with familiar cultural landmarks. Rather than speaking about cultural phenomena in abstract terms, media studies scholars use popular artifacts like TV shows and movies as vehicles to present difficult social issues. Whether or not we care to acknowledge it, media play an important role in our culture.

Media shape how we understand ourselves as well as our culture at large. As a media studies scholar myself, I have often encountered other thinkers and scholars who dismiss media studies as an illegitimate form of inquiry because we all seemingly have the capacity to consume and analyze media from our homes. Additionally, media scholars study the popular, and oftentimes the popular is dismissed as lowbrow or unintellectual. However, media studies isn't about simply *watching* or consuming media—it centers on peeling back the layers to understand how our own morals and values are shaped. Louise Byrne (2017) writes:

> Media studies is indeed often concerned with the popular, but that is one of its strengths. It is firmly grounded in society, in the communication, cultural understandings, concerns and sometimes even manipulation, of the mass of ordinary people. Long before anyone else, media studies was questioning the once utopian view of the internet, examining race and gender representation in the media and analysing the economic and

political power of the new media moguls. . . . Today, more than at any time since the invention of the first truly mass communication technology in the early 20th century, media are having a profound effect on our social, political and economic lives. As a result, media studies frequently takes an interdisciplinary approach to its enquiry, embracing politics, economics and psychology, as well as law and ethics.

In this chapter, I choose a specific film and three television shows to analyze because a) they are currently popular, and b) these media products propel a particular type of racialized commentary connected to the "zoologo-racial order," which is worth exploring for the purposes of this book. I did not cherry-pick this specific film or these shows to corroborate my arguments. During my training in graduate school, I learned that to be a successful media studies scholar, you have to critique the media you love the most. I am a fan of media and I regularly watch these shows for entertainment and enjoyment. (Seriously—you can quiz me about them if you ever meet me!)

While I was watching this film and these shows, I happened to take note of the ways in which race was employed and treated, and I then chose to bring them into this book. I begin with a brief analysis of one of my favorite Netflix comedy shows, *Santa Clarita Diet*. I then touch on *The Bachelor* franchise, and end with an extensive exploration of Jordan Peele's 2017 film *Get Out*. In order for my points to make sense, I have to provide some background for each of these, which may feel redundant if you've seen them before. Bear with me, dear reader, because it is necessary. I would also encourage you to watch the shows, episode, or film if you are not familiar with them.

Santa Clarita Diet

The Netflix horror-comedy show *Santa Clarita Diet*, starring Drew Barrymore, employs animal corpses as a signifier of white supremacy, which warrants an analysis that sets the tone for this entire chapter. Barrymore plays Sheila Hammond, a white suburban real estate agent who works with her husband, Joel. *Santa Clarita Diet* is a show that comically blurs the moral lines around eating sentient beings. After eating spoiled clams at a local Italian restaurant, Sheila dies and wakes up again as a zombie; the only thing she can now consume is human flesh. She tries to negotiate the violent aspects of her "diet" by only eating "bad" people. In fact, she states that Hitler would be her ideal person to consume. Although the show certainly provides commentary about morality and eating that warrants its own analysis from a vegan perspective, I found episode 3 of season 2 particularly interesting.

In this episode, titled "Moral Gray Area," Sheila and Joel end up unknowingly visiting the home of a white supremacist to negotiate getting a car back for a friend. After they knock on the door, a white man named Boone stands before them. He lets them inside his home despite not knowing them, stating that they look like "good white people." As Sheila and Joel cross the threshold, a taxidermied animal is strategically placed near the entrance and is the most prominent visual element in the space. As they continue to walk through the house, a camouflage-patterned hat is hanging from a door. Boone leads them to the living room and temporarily leaves so he can find the keys to the car. Boone's living room is decorated with the corpses of animals. He has two birds with their wings outstretched and pinned to the wall, and a taxidermied alligator's head on a bookshelf. Right above the alligator's head is a framed image of birds.

As they wait for Boone to return with the car keys, Joel takes the time to examine a cherrywood cabinet in the living room that happens to house a large amount of Nazi memorabilia: weapons, coffee mugs with swastikas on them, a copy of *Mein Kampf*, and bumper stickers that read WHITE POWER (see illustration on page 44). Sheila states: "The chances these are all gifts seem slim." They quickly conclude that Boone must be a Nazi, and as they come to this realization, the camera turns to Joel standing in front of a taxidermied buck's head mounted on the wall. As Boone re-enters the room with the car keys, the viewer can see a photo on the wall of a hunter (presumably Boone) wearing a camouflage hunting outfit and holding a gun.

Boone states: "Hey, you guys like fun, right? There's a funeral down the street for a gay, Jew, lady doctor. You wanna go shout stuff at her colored foster kids?"

At this point, one of Boone's friends enters the scene and attempts to sell Joel and Sheila raffle tickets for a Nazi softball team he's a part of. The friend stands in front of the Nazi cabinet and the taxidermied buck's head as he provides them with information about the racist team.

This episode comically pokes fun at a caricature of white supremacist neo-Nazis, and the producers accentuate this point by using taxidermy as part of the landscape. Taxidermy is a covert symbol of white supremacy. It does not conjure up the same cultural or emotional response as a swastika *per se*; however, it accomplishes the same racial goal: *to bolster the visibility of white supremacy*. Despite the fact that the actual scene doesn't dwell on the taxidermy in relation to racism, it is deliberately placed in the setting to accentuate the white-nationalist theme of Boone's characterization. It's not just a matter of Boone simply *collecting* taxidermy in his home, it's that this episode specifically shows us the anatomy of white supremacy by using animal corpses. As viewers, we are subconsciously invited to equate one's need to highlight one's ability to dominate "nature" with the desire to denigrate minoritized people.

In a modern Western context, taxidermy functions within the realm of white supremacist thought and attitude: "[T]axidermy is understood by some as the emblem of the very values that drove the imperialist spirit: 'dominion, courage, vigor, undaunted determination, triumph over the "untamed," and eventual victory' of patriarchal values" (Aloi 2018, 19).

Taxidermy is still celebrated today and is considered to be within white people's domain. Most of us in the U.S. have witnessed how particular white sub-cultures within the country rely upon camouflage clothing, hunting, animal corpses, guns, and taxidermy as part of the "uniform" for their white identity. These artifacts aren't necessarily a hundred-percent predictive but are correlated with certain social attitudes as well as "folkways and mores" (Sumner 1907).

In the episode "Moral Gray Area," the taxidermy becomes the first visual clue that Boone is racially violent. *Santa Clarita Diet* is a great place to start to build media literacy surrounding visual displays of zoological racism, and it sets the stage for a deeper analysis of how taxidermy and animal corpses serve as covert emblems of whiteness.

Taxidermy is also a prominent motif in the popular reality television show *The Bachelor*. (Yes, dear reader, I admit it: this progressive, woke-ass Black woman has covertly watched multiple seasons of *The Bachelor* and that guilty pleasure has finally paid off!) On the surface, *The Bachelor* may appear to have absolutely no significance for this book. However, having watched the ways in which race has been handled in each season, I realize that many unstated themes surrounding race and animality are inextricably linked to many of my points in this book.

The Structure of *The Bachelor*

Before explaining how taxidermy relates to *The Bachelor*, I must first explain how *The Bachelor* operates and guide you through the problematic racial elements that will serve as the framework for my analysis of taxidermy. *The Bachelor* is a reality TV dating game show that first aired in March 2002. The show's premise is this: one man, a bachelor, is in search of love, and twenty-five women compete to win his affection. At the end of every week, the bachelor holds a "rose ceremony" in which he hands out roses to the women who will continue on in the competition. Those women who don't receive roses are eliminated. If you win the final rose, the show usually concludes with a proposal from the bachelor.

Although *The Bachelor* may seem like yet another materialistic, superficial, heteronormative reality show about manufactured love, the racial dynamics that seek to secure white love are worth commenting on. *The Bachelor* is one of the most popular dating reality shows, with millions of viewers each season (Cooney 2018): "The . . . dating competition is among the most reliable weapons in ABC's programming arsenal, outrightly defying the Peak TV premise that only highbrow fare and buzzy streaming shows can capture the conversation" (Gonzalez 2017).

Just as the TV show *Judge Judy* injects ideas about right and wrong into our cultural imagination, *The Bachelor* shapes how we collectively understand love, romance, and desirability. Even though most progressive activists may scoff at the very mention of it, the show is worth examining because of its increasing popularity as well as its problematic relationship with racism. In the twenty-three seasons of the show, there has never been a nonwhite male bachelor. In 2012, *The Bachelor* franchise faced a class-action lawsuit for racial discrimination, which was eventually dismissed (Gardner 2012). Most of the nonwhite women who get a chance to compete for love are usually eliminated in the first few rounds.

This phenomenon is similar to the horror film trope of killing off the Black person first, which functions to keep the story and hero white. The killing is usually attributed to whatever "monster" is stalking the characters or whatever dangerous situation they are placed in, rather than being framed as a purposeful move on the part of the producers. Similarly, *The Bachelor* quickly eliminates the women of color who are brought on, and any charges of racism are pushed to the side in favor of a depoliticized, post-racial narrative that suggests they were removed because of matters of the heart, not matters of race. Although the bachelor as an individual certainly has the right to choose whomever he wants as a mate, my commentary is directed at the production of the show and the way that women of color are represented as undesirable and not worthy of being romantic partners.

Rachel Dubrofsky (2006) writes: "In *The Bachelor*, whiteness is an implicit prerequisite for finding a mate. Although many of the white women do not find love with the bachelor, they may be the center of the storyline for one or more episodes. . . . This is not the case for women of color, who work only to frame the narrative about white people forming a romantic union" (40).

The Bachelor's sister franchise, *The Bachelorette*, premiered in 2003. *The Bachelorette* has the same premise as *The Bachelor*, but instead of one man handing out roses to twenty-five women, one woman is selected to hand out roses to twenty-five men. *The Bachelor* and *The Bachelorette* alternate every season so that after *The Bachelor*'s season concludes, *The Bachelorette* premieres. The woman cast as the bachelorette is usually selected from the final four contestants from *The Bachelor*'s season. Out of thirteen seasons, only one woman of color has been selected to be the bachelorette.

In 2017, Rachel Lindsay, an African American lawyer, was cast as the first bachelorette of color; however, the show's viewership decreased. Commenting on the low ratings, Mike Fleiss, executive producer of the show, stated that he "found it incredibly disturbing in a Trumpish kind of way" (Harris 2018). In fact, there was a general air of racism surrounding Rachel's entire season, exemplified by a former *Bachelor* contestant who tweeted that when she turned on Rachel Lindsay's season of *The Bachelorette*, she thought she was watching *Love and Hip Hop*, a reality television show that centers on popular hip hop stars (French 2017).

ZooLogo-Racial Necrophilia and Animal Death as Symbolism of White Power

Just as the election of Donald Trump could be perceived as a racial backlash to Barack Obama's presidency, one could argue that there was a racial backlash to *The Bachelor* franchise after Rachel Lindsay's season. Rather than carrying the mantle of racial progress by selecting a bachelor of color after Rachel's season concluded, in 2018 the producers selected a white man named Arie Luyendyk Jr. as the new bachelor with a mostly white pool of female contestants. As Rachel Dubrofsky writes: "[T]he show's racism is not overt. At times it is difficult to pin down. This is what [cultural theorist Stuart] Hall calls 'inferential racism': when racist representations are unspoken and naturalized, making the racist premises upon which the representations rely difficult to bring to the surface" (42).

Of course, most of the nine minoritized women featured on Arie's season (out of twenty-nine women in total) were eliminated in the first few rounds. One of the women introduced at the beginning of the show was a white woman with blond hair named Kendall Long. She was introduced as a "quirky" girl who loved taxidermy. In fact, during her introductory promotional video, she played ukulele and sang to a taxidermied sea lion.[1] Throughout the season, she constantly referred to taxidermy and her love of collecting animal corpses. She succeeded in becoming one of the three women in the final, which made her eligible to become the bachelorette. In fact, all three women who made it to the end were white.

In *The Bachelor* enterprise, the final four women in the competition get an opportunity to take the bachelor to their hometowns to introduce him to their families. *The Bachelor* franchise is quite formulaic in that the hometown episodes often begin with the bachelor and the contestant going on a very produced date before meeting the family. Normally, this takes the form of the bachelor and the contestant taking a romantic stroll through a park, getting a quick bite to eat, or visiting a location from the contestant's youth that has significance to her.

During Kendall's hometown date, she does something uncharacteristic by taking Arie to a large warehouse with taxidermied animals on display. She states: "We are actually going to be mounting some taxidermy of our own." They walk into a room in which two deflated rat corpses lie on a table. As they are stuffing the rat skins, Kendall states: "In a way, taxidermy is like a perfect relationship, because it's something that's going to last forever."

They dress the two rats up in wedding attire. Arie holds the male rat dressed in a groom's outfit and asks, "Kendall, will you accept this rose?" She holds up her rat in a wedding dress and replies, "Yes, I will." They make the taxidermied rats kiss and place them in a small display with an image of the Eiffel Tower behind them. Arie tells Kendall that if she advances in the competition, "she could have her little room where she does taxidermy, and I'll have my garage where I work on cars. . . ."

In this particular season, taxidermy seems like a random activity, chalked up to the bizarre habits of one woman who describes herself as "weird." However, when we look at *The Bachelor* enterprise as a vehicle for recuperating and promoting segregated romance, white love, and white normalcy, this act of taxidermy takes on a more insidious character.

The fact that the taxidermied rats are used as symbols to discuss white love and are used to act out *The Bachelor*'s rose ceremony demonstrates the multidimensional displays of whiteness on the show. Rat corpses become vehicles to enact white fantasies of love, conjuring up themes of what I would call zoological ventriloquism whereby nonhuman bodies and corpses are used as props. I find this to be quite significant, especially because in this season it appears as though the producers were attempting to revive the whiteness that the franchise lost when Rachel Lindsay became the bachelorette (Barnes 2017).

The emphasis on taxidermy in this season, with the backdrop of white supremacy and white unity, bolsters the point I'm making: that taxidermy isn't just a random activity reserved for quirky people who love nature, but rather it exists as a symbol of white supremacy and white domination. "'[T]axidermy' may be conceptualized as a sign system inclusive of but not restricted to the literal stuffing of skins that reproduces a continually rearticulating network of signs that manipulate the categories of humans and animals, culture and nature, and life and death in the service of white supremacy" (Wakeham 2008, 6).

Using corpses as vehicles to celebrate white love can exist only on the operating table of racist necrophilia, which is a cornerstone of white supremacy (Curry 2016, 485). Racist necrophilia is white supremacy's insatiable, sexual desire for Black death. We can think of the murders of Terrance Rankins and Eric Glover, two twenty-two-year-old Black men, in 2013 (*Daily Mail* Reporter 2015). The men were lured into a home in Joliet, Illinois, under the pretense of a party and were robbed and murdered by four white people: Joshua Miner (twenty-four years old), Adam Landerman (nineteen years old), Alisa Massaro (eighteen years old), and Bethany McKee (eighteen years old).

After the murders, Miner, Landerman, and Massaro decided to have a threesome on top of the corpses. The murders have been called "Nightmare on Hickory Street" (Gray 2018). These acts are not the doing of people who are just generally necrophiliac or "evil" but of ultra-conformists to a culture that sexualizes the brutalization of Blackness.

I am extending this concept of racist necrophilia to account for white supremacy's sexual, racist appetite for *nonhuman* death, since animals are racialized subjects in the extant racial order.[2] In its 2018 season, *The Bachelor* relied upon taxidermic racial tropes and racist necrophilia to secure the whiteness of the show. This is how the zoologo-racial order operates to maintain *white* order. Taxidermy-ing animals is projecting a racialized power fantasy onto the given objects.

Just as in the *Santa Clarita Diet* episode "Moral Gray Area," taxidermy is used as a covert symbol for bolstering white supremacy and white unity in *The Bachelor*. Rather than overtly announcing that they were attempting to revive the whiteness of the show after Rachel's season, *The Bachelor*'s producers saturated Arie's season with signifiers of whiteness: from casting half of the contestants with bright blond hair to orchestrating a romantic date in a taxidermy warehouse. The animal corpses served as racial signposts to reassure viewers that their show was white again.

From Taxidermy-ing to Metabolizing "Nonhuman" Bodies and Souls

Racism as Zoological Witchcraft

One of the most pernicious elements of white supremacy is its ability to consume the bodies and essences of the oppressed. We are accustomed to reading about native/indigenous cultures that engaged in practices of cannibalism (Rose 2014); however, we are beginning to also learn about the history of white colonizers consuming their victims. James W. Perkinson (2005) writes:

> The basic theme is that American identity and history are profoundly informed by an ongoing interweaving of white entitlement and black disenfranchisement, together articulating the basic framework within which other ethnic groups negotiate their cultural differences and jockey for position in the social hierarchy of the country. The basic political conviction is that, historically, white supremacy is the child of Christian supremacy, and that contemporary American notions of its own global supremacy (that have emerged especially since World War II) are the offspring of both. The core argument is that European (and subsequent American) race discourse can be ironically understood as modernity's "witchcraft practice"—in fact, if not in name, leveraging and licensing an

ongoing project of plunder that is effectively consuming (or in witchcraft terms, "eating") the substance of the rest of the globe. (xxiii)

Being "consumable" becomes a marker of zoological oppression: "Within plantation culture, this culture of consumption took the form of whites literally flaying and smoking African American flesh and overt references in slave narratives to masters literally and metaphorically consuming their slaves" (Woodard 2014, 12). Black people were regarded as consumable fleshy items to be ingested and/or materially repurposed by white supremacy.

In *The Delectable Negro*, Vincent Woodard shares the story of Nat Turner, who led a slave rebellion in Virginia on November 11, 1831, that left around fifty-five white people dead. As punishment, Turner was lynched. Although many people learn about Nat Turner's rebellion in grade school, most are not familiar with the fact that after his lynching, he was decapitated, skinned, and then materially repurposed into different items: "The money purse made of Turner's skin and the grease made from his boiled-down flesh convey the limitless consumptive uses of the slave and the myriad ways in which the ruling class could satiate unspoken desires and taste for Negro flesh" (172).

Whites also boiled down Turner's flesh to a liquid that they ingested as a medicinal substance (65). In a 2016 *New York Times* story, a history teacher shared a moment in her African American history class in which one of her white students confessed that his family still owned a purse that was composed partially of Black flesh. The purse had been handed down through his family and it was soon going to be his. The dominant class routinely consumed Black bodies, and many slave narratives echo this reality (Berry 2016).

In his memoir, Olaudah Equiano, a formerly enslaved African and campaigner for abolition, shares how he was kidnapped in 1789 and taken to the Caribbean where he was sold as a slave. Fearing what his fate would be, he confided in the other enslaved Africans: "I asked them if we were not to be eaten by those white men with horrible looks, red faces and loose hair. They told me I was not. But still I feared I should be put to death, the white people looked and acted, as I thought, in so savage a manner; for I had never seen among any people such instances of brutal cruelty" (International Slavery Museum).

Enslaved Africans had a legitimate reason to fear the cannibalistic nature of whites, considering that white people often consumed the bodies of slaves. Equiano actually refers to overseers as "human butchers." Slaves were also whipped until raw, and overseers would rub pepper and salt onto their bodies. Others would cut off their ears, broil them, and feed them to other slaves as punishment (Woodard 2014, 46). The physical violence Black folks experienced at the hands of those in the dominant class was made possible only because they were conceptually considered nonhuman.

As I've stated throughout my work, conceptual violence precedes physical violence. You must be *thought of* as an inferior subject before your body is used, abused, manipulated, and consumed. This is evident in nonhuman animal oppression. Before animals are stuffed into zoos or turned into taxidermied pieces to be mounted on walls, they are conceptually conceived of as bodies designed for compulsory elimination.

Earlier in this chapter, I brought in an analysis of taxidermy that demonstrated how this practice is not just about displaying animal corpses on walls but is simultaneously a display of power and racial value systems.

To have the power to ingest someone's soul and to re-stuff their essence with your own is one of the unique tenets of racial terrorism. The ways in which the dominant class gets to determine whose life matters and whose doesn't, as well as who is human and who is animal, constitute a zoological sport. It's important to note that I see a convergence between Claire Jean Kim's work on the zoological dimensions of racism and James W. Perkinson's scholarship constructing European race discourse itself as a kind of witchcraft practice. I call this theoretical convergence "zoological witchcraft." Perkinson is deliberately comparing racist white Christian consumptive activities with the way that "primitive" shamanistic witchcraft often employs "soul eating" to attack or gain power over another: "U.S. slavery was a form of social cannibalism. . . . [W]hites were becoming, unbeknown to themselves, the very cannibalistic types that they feared and project upon every strange land and people they encountered" (Woodard 2014, 66).

White supremacist zoological witchcraft is a practice whereby the minoritized class is physically and conceptually consumed and "stuffed" with definitions from the dominant class. The dominant class has the ability and the means to "get inside" and tamper with the essence of the Other, reducing them to epidermal shells and props. The goal is to render Black consciousness extinct while making the Black body or epidermal shell increasingly visible.[3] Minoritized bodies serve as hollowed-out shells that become emblems of white supremacist superiority, which are displayed to showcase racial degradation.

In the U.S., lynching was a unique form of racial terrorism that was used to demonstrate the colonial mastery of those in the dominant class. The vulgarity of lynching wasn't visible only in the violent physical crime itself but also in its aftermath. Bones from Black bodies were often displayed in local shops (Lartey 2018). Black bodies became souvenirs; body parts were distributed amongst townsfolk (Young 2005).

In *Without Sanctuary: Lynching Photography in America* (2000), Leon F. Litwack details the lynching of Sam Hose, a Black man who lived in Georgia. After he was chained to a tree and burned alive, his heart and liver were removed and the "crowd fought over these souvenirs" (9). Someone reportedly delivered a slice of Sam's heart to the governor of Georgia. Litwack shares the thoughts of a Black Mississippian in the 1930s who stated: "They had a license to kill anything but a nigger. We was always in season" (Litwack 2000, 12).

The phrase *always in season* became the title for the 2019 documentary I worked on as an associate producer. The film, directed by Jacqueline Olive, discusses the history of lynching in the U.S. as well as the ways in which Black bodies are still mutilated and animalized in contemporary society. The routine brutalization of Black bodies through white racial rituals like lynching demonstrates the different ways in which Black bodies were and are consumed. Woodard (2014) writes:

> This desire was less about literal consumption and more about the cultivated taste the white person developed for the African. Whites often satiated this taste and appetite through acts of violence, sexual exploitation, imagined ingestion of the black, or through staged rituals designed to incrementally harvest black spirit and soul. The delectability of the black person was of course a factor in literal flesh consumption, but my main point . . . is that literal cannibalism always occurred within cultural, ideological contexts. (459)

Woodard shares the story of George, a young enslaved Black man who endured ritualized racial violence at the hands of Lilburn Lewis, a white Kentuckian slave owner. George was sent to a spring to collect water in a pitcher; he accidentally dropped the pitcher, which shattered into pieces. As punishment, "his master bound him to a wooden plank and in the manner of a butcher, quartered him with an axe and cooked his severed body parts and pieces of flesh over a billowing fire" (59). George's master forced the other enslaved Africans to watch, in hopes of teaching them a lesson: "As parasite and consumer, the master takes in, imbibes George's essence; George's terror and the terror of all the slaves feed the master's authority and power. And we have to consider that in addition to emotional and spiritual consumption, the master might have literally ingested pieces of George's flesh" (61).

White supremacy's cannibalistic cravings became so strong that simply collecting Black bodies as souvenirs or displaying them as emblems of colonial mastery wasn't fulfilling. Black muscle needed to be **transmogrified** into a machine—a vehicle those in the dominant class could use to carry out their witchcraft practices and continue the legacy of white domination. When I say "witchcraft," I am not refer-encing its popular conception (as in, for example, the Salem witchcraft trials). I am arguing that white supremacist witchcraft practices were on par with tribalistic, superstitious justifications for killing, eating, raping, and sacrificing humans. From past to present, the West has employed both pseudo-science and the scientific establishment to support their ideas.

In Haitian culture, *bokers* are witchcraft practitioners who suck out and instill another's essence in the *zombie astral*: "The *zombi* [*sic*] *astral* differs from the *zombi cadavre*, in that the *zombi astral* does not require a corpse. Instead of a dead body being reanimated as it is with the *zombi cadavre*, it is the soul or consciousness of a person being captured in a vessel in order to enhance the power of the one who captured it" (Brown 2018b).

White supremacy is a zoological witchcraft mechanism that seeks to ingest the essence of minoritized people and reanimate their bodies with white supremacist projections and fantasies. It's important to ensure that we turn the gaze back onto whiteness in relation to the sorcery inherent in white people's own racial practices:

> Witchcraft emerges in colonial perspective and practice as a structuring device that mediates meanings of "European order" and "indigenous disorder." . . . Ironically, colonial politics seeking to suppress native practices demarcated as "witchcraft," in effect, accomplish the same kind of differentiation and expla-nation. The very charge of "witchcraft practice" can be itself understood as a form of witchcraft." (Perkinson 2004, 606–7)

Just as other cultures may have witchcraft practitioners, one could argue that white supremacy *itself* is a unique form of witchcraft anchored to colonialism, Christianity, plunder, and consumption. Woodard (2014) writes:

It was one thing for whites to draw upon Christian theology as a means of justifying their consumptive rituals and appetites and an altogether different matter for them to use Christian theology and social ritual as a means of feeding and sustaining self and social stature. Africans throughout the continent frequently equated European Christianity with human consumption. (48)

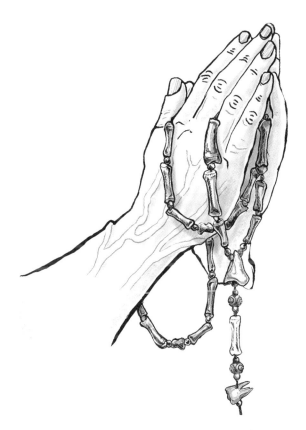

White supremacy's sorcery is its ability to define the entire world from white people's standpoint and to affect the internal psyches of other living beings. Not only does this have physical repercussions, it also causes severe multigenerational psychological damage to the oppressed. Double consciousness, a social/psychological condition coined by W. E. B. Du Bois in *The Souls of Black Folk*, is characterized by a fractured consciousness whereby the oppressed see the world through our own eyes as well as through the eyes of the oppressor. We are constantly experiencing inner turmoil, grappling with our inferiority, and perpetually coexisting with an internal voice that tells us we are not human. Double consciousness could be considered a symptom of white supremacist shamanism, or the ability to get inside—to disturb and hijack—the essence and the consciousness of another.

Get Out

The framing of white supremacy as a consumptive witchcraft practice serves as the storyline for the popular film *Get Out*, directed by Jordan Peele. *Get Out* is described as a social thriller because it treats racism, rather than a ghost or zombie, as the scary entity. The film follows the protagonist, Chris Washington (pictured at the top of page 61), a talented African American photographer who is in a relationship with a white woman named Rose Armitage (pictured on page 66). The film begins with Chris preparing to meet Rose's parents for the first time; naturally, he has some reservations considering that Rose has not yet informed them that he is Black.

In the opening scenes, Chris is in his apartment getting ready for the day after taking a shower. His mirror is fogged up from the condensation and he cleans it with a towel. The scene then switches to a pastry shop where Rose is gleefully perusing an assortment of pastries, trying to decide which to purchase and consume. The scene shifts back to Chris in his bathroom, applying white shaving cream to his face. He takes the razor and begins shaving, only to cut his neck. These two scenes are visually significant because Rose's consumptive behaviors are displayed at the same time we are introduced to Chris's vulnerability.

When Chris and Rose are driving to her parents' house, Rose accidentally hits a female deer with her car. Although Rose is visibly upset that they got into an accident, she does not appear to demonstrate any concern for the deer, whereas Chris takes the time to go over and check on her. This serves as the first racial omen in the film. When they arrive at Rose's parents' house, Chris and Rose explain their delay to her parents. In response, Dean, Rose's father, states: "You know what I say? I say one down, a couple hundred thousand to go. I don't mean to get on my high horse, but I'm telling you, I do not like the deer. I'm sick of it; they're taking over. They're like rats. They're destroying the ecosystem. I see a dead deer on the side of the road and I think, 'That's a start.'"

Viewers may think Dean is referring only to literal deer, but it becomes obvious as the plot progresses that this comment has racial undertones. In fact, most people of color are accustomed to hearing about Black and Brown people "taking over" white communities in much the same way. This fear of white human territories being "taken over" or encroached on has become the basis for many instances in which white people have called the police on Black and Brown citizens who are seen as being threatening or not belonging.

I'm reminded of an event in 2018 in which a twelve-year-old Black boy named Reggie Fields was cutting grass in his neighborhood and an unidentified neighbor called the police on him. That same year, a fifteen-year-old Black teen was swimming at a pool in South Carolina when a white woman called the police and assaulted the teen by striking him in the face and chest (Molina 2018). Our presence is framed as analogous to a natural disaster that threatens the white human ecology, and thus we must be removed or violently exterminated. This narrative works to naturalize white humans as the dominant and natural citizens of the Earth.

During his stay at the Armitages', Chris begins to feel uneasy as he notices bizarre actions on the part of the Black staff and Rose's family. The viewer is introduced to Georgina, the Black maid, whose giddy and unnaturally happy disposition starts to make Chris uncomfortable, especially because there are moments in which her speech has a tense undertone. (See illustration on page 105). Walter, the Black groundskeeper, mirrors Georgina's unnaturally happy attitude and often speaks in an antiquated style. In reference to Rose, Walter states that she's "one of a kind. Top of the line. A real doggone keeper." Additionally, Chris begins to notice that Walter aimlessly sprints at night in the front yard of the Armitage family home.

Chris's suspicions are further intensified after he wakes up late one night and sits across from Rose's mother, Missy (picured below), who wants to perform hypnotherapy on him to help him stop smoking.

Missy begins stirring her spoon in her tea and starts asking Chris personal questions about his life, such as his emotions on the day his mother passed away. After engaging with Missy's questions, Chris becomes paralyzed and his consciousness is separated from his body.

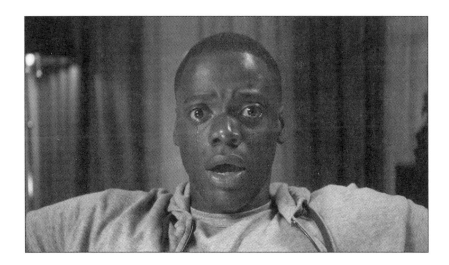

He wakes up the next morning without a desire to smoke and assumes that the hypnotism was successful. However, he has no memory of the event.

That same day, the Armitages throw a party at which several of their friends show up. At this party, Chris meets a young Black man named Logan (pictured below, left).

Logan is dressed in a suit and tie, along with a hat. An elderly white woman clings to Logan's arm most of the time, suggesting that they are a couple. Chris approaches Logan in hopes that he might find some solidarity with another Black person among all of the white guests. However, it becomes apparent that like Walter and Georgina, this young man also speaks in an antiquated style, which makes Chris uneasy.

In fact, Logan racially betrays Chris by informing the guests that "Chris was just telling me how much more comfortable he was with me being here":

> In each of these interactions, Georgina, Walter and Logan seem eerie in part because there's a mismatch between what Chris sees when he looks at them, and what he hears when they open their mouths. (Rosenberg 2017)

At one point, guests are standing outside and Chris takes a photograph of Logan with his cell phone; however, he forgets to turn off the flash. The flash alters Logan's entire personality. His face is overcome with fear and he rushes toward Chris while his nose starts to bleed. He repeatedly yells, "Get out!" The white guests grab Logan and take him inside to visit with Missy. Chris is visibly shaken by this event, which only adds to his suspicion that something odd is going on at this house. Chris calls his friend, Rod Williams (pictured right), a TSA agent who serves as comedic relief throughout the film.

Rod warns Chris about the Armitages and even suggests that they might be kidnapping Black people to turn them into sex slaves: "Bruh, how you not scared of this, man?" says Rod. "White people love making people sex slaves and shit."

The viewer eventually learns that the Armitages are a part of an insidious racial cult that kidnaps Black people, hypnotizes them, and steals their bodies for its own gain. The consciousness/essence of Black people is sent to "the sunken place," where they are suspended in dark space and become "passengers" in their bodies:

The film represents the sunken place literally: it materializes a black cosmic hole that Chris's body falls through as he witnesses reality at a remove. . . . Chris's body goes rigid and his eyes widen; like Walter and Georgina, he's not quite there. (Da Costa 2017)

Black bodies are auctioned off to club members. After purchasing the body, the buyer undergoes a process the Armitages call the "coagula," whereby their brain is implanted into the Black person's skull where they can control the Black body. The Black person becomes a vessel for white consciousness, a mere biological puppet for white fantasies and desires. The viewer learns that Georgina and Walter are actually Rose's grandparents. The two Black bodies that serve as the vehicles for their brains belong to two Black people (their real names are never revealed) who were kidnapped and forced to undergo the coagula surgery. Chris also learns that Logan is actually a man named Andre Hayworth, who went missing a few months prior.

Some elements of *Get Out* are inescapably linked to the obvious history of white racial terrorism. In the Armitages' basement, a taxidermied bust of a buck is mounted on the wall. The term *buck* is a racial slur that was historically used to refer to unruly Black men. In addition, as I have already demonstrated, taxidermy is often employed to make white supremacy visible. *Get Out* is the first racial film I have seen in which animals aren't just a metaphor for the violence people of color experience. Jordan Peele shows us how animals are *simultaneously* a casualty of white supremacist violence.

Peele demonstrates how white supremacy is maintained by anti-Black zoological attitudes and that a cornerstone of white supremacy is its fetishistic desire to consume the oppressed. He shows us a multi-dimensional white supremacy that reflects what Kim (2017) calls the "zoologo-racial order" (10). There is a rich history through which to track the consumptive desires of white supremacy as an exercise of colonial mastery and power:

> Most . . . examples of consumption, on and off the plantation, range from the literal murder and eating of black persons to what we might think of as metaphoric acts. I refer to these metaphoric acts—which encompass starving, flesh-seasoning rituals, and sexual modes of consumption—variously as consumption, human consumption, metaphoric consumption, instance of social consumption, and even cannibalism. (Woodard 2014, 6)

Peele's usage of taxidermy as a white supremacist trope relies upon the literal and metaphorical act of consumption. Animals are stuffed and hang from the wall—frozen, eternal reminders of white supremacy's ruthlessness. The white people at the Armitages' also engage in re-stuffing the essences of Black people to bolster their own superiority and longevity.

Black people become mere epidermal shells for the ruling class. Our consciousnesses are ingested and metabolized in the bellies of white fantasies; our essences serve as fuel for the white cult members. This is the sunken place. After our souls are taken, all we have left are empty shells ripe for stuffing and a collection of limp muscles that we can no longer control. Taxidermied animals serve as racial signposts of what's to come for Black visitors to the town. *Get Out* is not just about Black people becoming "zombies," as a lot of sources suggest. It's that there's a *zoological* component to this racial zombification, or what I introduced earlier as zoological witchcraft.

In *Get Out*, white supremacy is framed as a zoological witchcraft practice: the white people and the one Asian guest[4] engage in racial rituals anchored to stripping the Black body of its essence and repurposing it to empower their own fantasies. When Chris tries to escape from the Armitage home at the end of the film, he quickly learns that Rose is a part of the cult and that part of her job was to lure him to the home under the guise of meeting her parents.

Chris tries to escape; Missy sends Chris to the sunken place through hypnosis, which is a nod to white supremacist shamanism. He becomes paralyzed and falls to the ground. Chris is taken to the basement and bound by what appear to be leather belts attached to a leather chair.[5] The Armitages play a video on a television placed in front of Chris to explain to him what the coagula is. Right above the television is a mounted taxidermied buck's head seemingly gazing at Chris. At this moment, Chris learns that the Armitages will surgically operate on his brain and Jim Hudson, a blind white man who purchased Chris's body at a silent auction, will have his brain transplanted into Chris's skull. Chris's body will be used as a vehicle for Jim's brain. Jim's face then appears on the television as he prepares for the surgery and he tries to dialogue with Chris.

Chris asks Jim why they are specifically hunting Black people for this project and Jim replies: "Who knows? People want to change. Some people want to be stronger . . . faster . . . cooler. Black is in fashion." Black skin becomes a fashion statement, a piece of trendy corpse skin like leather or fur. Blackness can exist in a white supremacist climate only as a vehicle for white people's fantasies.

It's not a coincidence that Rose (pictured left) deliberately hunts for Black people who possess particular talents or are successful in their careers. Black success is a threat to the racial status quo (Clegg 2018). Chris is a successful and creative photographer. The viewer learns that Rose is already hunting for her next Black victim. She searches on her laptop for successful players in the National Basketball Association. Her sexual thirst for Black bodies and Black social death helps keep the violent, racist, zoological, necrophiliac system alive:

> The origins of the U.S. culture of consumption trace back to the first contact between European colonizers and coastal Africans. By the early twentieth century, even Europeans admitted to and documented a connection between European global expansion and a sexual/libidinal appetite for African flesh. (Woodard 2014, 309)

In *Get Out*, Black people are trapped in a perpetual act of white supremacist zoological ventriloquism. White people in the film don't mind sharing space with Black people, so long as Black people are stripped of their context and forced to endure grotesque psychological and physical abuse. Rather than forcing Black folks into slavery or servitude, the white people in *Get Out* construct an entirely new, sadistic form of social death whereby Black people are forced to become passengers in their own bodies. Just as Dean hates deer, yet has a taxidermied buck's head mounted on his wall, the visibility of Blackness is integral to white people because the bodies serve as constant reminders of their own superiority and colonial mastery. They get to enact violence on Black bodies while simultaneously seeming benevolent to Black people by subscribing to integrationist illusions in which Blackness is hyper-represented but Black consciousness is rendered extinct.[6]

Black bodies become vehicles the ruling class can flaunt, like fancy cars that the wealthy use as signifiers of their success. In this sense, one becomes racially successful by virtue of selecting which Black body one wants to purchase and shapeshift into. In fact, Jordan Peele confirmed that he purposely made the Armitages' friends all arrive at the gathering in black cars as a symbolic nod to the ways in which Black bodies are used as vehicles in the film (*Vanity Fair* 2017).

It's important to note the ritualistic aesthetics of Dean Armitage's surgery room, where he performs the coagula surgery. Among surgical equipment and other items one would expect to find in a doctor's office are four candles strategically placed around the room, conjuring up themes of racial shamanism and witchcraft.

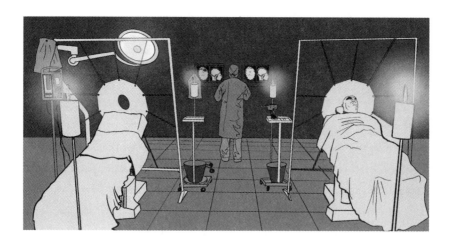

Racial oppression becomes a religious ritual for Rose's family whereby they desire Black flesh in order for their own racial potential to blossom. In fact, Rose's father actually tells Chris: "Even the sun will die someday. But, we are divine. We are the gods trapped in cocoons. . . ." In this sense, viewers can witness an interesting contradiction: Black people are seen as subhuman, but the white people in *Get Out* cannot reach their "divine" potential without Black bodies:

> When black Americans described instances of the eating, cooking, and consumption of flesh in slave narratives, newspaper articles, speeches, testimonials, sermons, and autobiographies, they not only questioned the national body politic but also tried to understand why and how they had become so delectable, so erotically appetizing, to a nation and white populace that, at least rhetorically, denied and despised their humanity. (Woodard 2014, 8)

The Black people in *Get Out* aren't petrified corpses preserved on a wall; they aren't just sleepwalking. They are "tried on" as racialized suits, consumed, and sexually violated. They become interactive taxidermic vehicles. In her essay for *Harper's* magazine, Zadie Smith (2017) writes: "The white people in *Get Out* want to get inside the Black experience: They want to wear it like a skin and walk around in it. The modern word for this is 'appropriation.'" However, *appropriation* doesn't really capture the zoological dimensions of racism. Instead, white people's insatiable, racist, cannibalistic desires for Black bodies function as a form of zoological racist necrophilia: a sexual appetite for Black flesh coupled with a wish to see Black people both literally and discursively *dead*.

When Chris is bound to the leather seat in the basement, he tries to escape. He rips the skin of the leather seat with his fingers, and cotton stuffing emerges.

Although several critics have noted the significance of the cotton (in reference to slavery), the profound act of revealing the white stuffing from inside the *leather* (cow skin) chair exposes the multidimensional and multi-textured nature of white supremacy, which is valuable for the conversation about animality, racism, and taxidermy. All too often, we as a culture notice only the obvious markers of white supremacy, but to get to the root of this system, we have to realize that even the raw materials matter.

The fact that Chris is forced to wear leather shackles and sit on a chair covered in leather *matters*. We can't discuss the racial violence Chris experiences without exploring how the entire scene is saturated with expressions of white supremacist zoological violence. These animal parts are not merely the backdrop to the main storyline . . . they *are* the storyline. When Chris is bound to the chair with leather belts, he is also deliberately seated across from the buck stuffed and mounted on the wall. Just like the buck, Chris is about to become taxidermied.

This isn't about appropriation or white folks wanting to temporarily "become" Black people. This is about a desire to metabolize Blackness while wearing Black people's muscles and skin as an emblem of racial superiority and white tribalistic ritual:

European forms of colonization and their neoliberal American successors beg analysis as the most ruthless realization of sorcery in history, a clandestine and complex "whitening" of the practices of plunder that ends up effectively hiding those practices most of all from the practitioners themselves. The witch can no longer recognize itself in the mirror of witchery. (Perkinson 2005, xxv)

Our muscles and our skin are detached from our bodies to ensure the comfort of white supremacy. Just as cow skin covers the chair, Black skin becomes the wallpaper for white fantasies. This isn't a commentary on how animal oppression and Black oppression are "the same," but how "both groups were smuggled onto a racial hierarchy that the dominant class created to naturalize their own superiority and the inferiority of everyone else" (*VeganLife* 2017).

Despite the fact that *Get Out* is saturated with markers of white supremacy as a zoological consumptive machine, most think pieces and blogs that have attempted to discuss the brilliance of Jordan Peele's film have completely left out a deeper analysis of white supremacy and how its violence against animals *itself* serves as an expression of racism. The consumption of animals is so routine and normalized that even scholars and thinkers who politicize the colonial consumption of marginalized bodies do not realize how they are still participating in the legacy of coloniality by ignoring the institutionalized suffering of animals. As thinkers and activists, we can keep pointing out how cruel the consumption of Black and Brown bodies is; however, this phenomenon will never stop manifesting itself until we deal with the root of the behavior, which requires us to realize that animal experiences are the invisible framework keeping colonial consumption intact.

Some critics of *Get Out* have used the language of "trophies" to describe the racial victims in the film but have not commented on animals as casualties of white supremacist violence. The *Los Angeles Times* was one of the few publications to point out how a particular scene involving milk in the film is a visual demonstration of racism (Yamato 2017). Rose separates her colored cereal from her white milk, which is significant, especially since milk has become the staple beverage of the alt-right (Gambert 2018).

How is it possible that we live in an era in which anti-racist activists are acutely aware of how white supremacy treats people of color "like animals," but are discouraged from examining how literal animals are casualties of this racial caste system as well? This signals that the mainstream theories we have been using to understand racial oppression might be tainted with Eurocentric logic. In order to liberate ourselves, we must re-examine the tools we are using to "fight" the system to help us see the full territory of white supremacy.

3

Moving from Intersectionality to Multidimensional Liberation Theory

I want to emphasize categorical, dichotomous, hierarchical logic as central to modern, colonial, capitalist thinking about race, gender and sexuality.—**Maria Lugones** (2010, 742)

I . . . prefer multidimensionality because it more effectively captures the inherent complexity and irreversibly multilayered nature of everyone's identities and of oppression. . . .
—**Darren Lenard Hutchinson** (1997, 641)

DESPITE THE FACT THAT WE ARE CAN QUITE FLUENTLY DISCUSS HOW terms like *animal* feed into our own dehumanization as people of color, there isn't a lot of mainstream encouragement for us to *actually extend the conversation to the ways in which animality is the foundation of the racial system.* We can't possibly advocate a liberatory racial politics while ignoring the brutal slaughter of nonhuman animals and how their bodies have been used as sites of racial exploitation and consumption.

Animals have always served as a metaphor for us to talk about the racial violence we experience as people of color; however, we need to take the next step and acknowledge that they are casualties of white supremacist violence as well. They are casualties of the project of "animality," which is historically and contemporarily part of our own condition. This acknowledgment isn't a comparison; it is recognition that white supremacy's ruthlessness isn't limited to people of color.

I would argue that the reason why people are often immediately dismissive of the conversation about race and animals (and the reason why many anti-racist activists don't even notice animals as victims of white supremacist violence) is because we have a limited and *revised* understanding of white supremacy that ignores the history of zoological frameworks being utilized to bolster the ruling class's superiority. As I mentioned in the Introduction, we have been trained as activists to categorize the world into different "filing cabinets." We have been trained to think about the world using certain theories and frameworks that may not be providing the full picture.

Intersectionality has become the dominant theory used in almost every mainstream social justice movement today, but this theory limits our ability to understand how vast the landscape of racism is. Even though it has also become quite common to critique intersectionality (in part because of the rise of anti–"social justice warrior" narratives),[1] I offer a critique of intersectionality that actually takes into consideration the well-being of the oppressed. Intersectionality is not the best social theory model to capture how incredibly messy and complex oppression is, and I believe this critique of intersectionality is necessary, especially because so many activists are adding animal experiences to the intersectional matrix of oppressions without a second thought. Throwing so many oppressions into the mix without a proper framework only muddles the conversation further.

The Limits of Intersectionality Theory in Progressive Social Movements

Whenever I give talks or interviews about the tension between animal rights and anti-racism, I am usually asked the following question: "If Black Lives Matter won't acknowledge animal oppression, and if the animal rights movement won't acknowledge racism, should we just make these two movements intersect to solve the problem?"

Think about that for a minute: If one movement that doesn't recognize the full scope and size of the problem intersects with another movement that also doesn't recognize the scope and size of the problem, should we make them converge? Will that really provide us with new insights? I can't tell you how many times I've been asked this question or some derivative form of it. To a certain extent, I completely understand why "intersectionality" seems logical in this instance. Intersectionality is seductive because it takes seemingly disparate oppressions and forces them into the same conversational space, which can make it seem as though the oppressions are "communicating" with one another. So if we feel as though a particular social movement isn't talking about an issue, we think it makes sense to just throw that issue into the mix. But it is easy to dilute issues when you start throwing all oppressions together *without a proper framework* to handle all of those oppressions. When you don't have a proper framework, we start rattling off oppressions, as we do items on a checklist, with no analysis attached. It becomes a very hollow form of verbal or rhetorical activism.

Making Black Lives Matter connect to the animal rights movement presupposes that each movement is sound in its approach and analysis of the problems at hand. I think Black Lives Matter is a great movement, but it tends to have a narrow, one-dimensional take on racism; the animal rights movement also has a narrow, one-dimensional take on animal oppression. On top of that, I don't believe a real intersection or connection ever takes place.

In 2016, I stated that intersectionality feels more like *social layerism*—a term I use to describe how oppressions are piled on top of one another though they never truly intersect. In other words, whereas activists mention more and more oppressions in the same sentence, the oppressions don't really have a relationship with one another. This means you may encounter activists who say something like "We need to dismantle speciesism, and racism, and sexism, and transphobia, and ableism," but there isn't a deeper analysis to explain how these social phenomena relate to one another. Because the oppressions are all loaded on top of one another, they give the illusion that a robust and substantial structure stands before you, yet they are all disconnected, individual pieces that are not fused: nothing holds them together.

In trying to "connect" movements (like animal rights and Black Lives Matter), we are also implicitly acknowledging that each movement is limited in some way. This means we must address the *knowledge that informs our understanding of what oppression is rather than trying to fix the problem at the movement level.* We don't need movements to intersect; we need new imaginations of how oppressions manifest themselves at the root. Once again, the project I'm advocating goes much deeper than "connections" and "intersections"; I'm fighting for activists to revolutionize how they understand oppression itself.

Allow me to draw an analogy to further illustrate my point. Let's say you are sitting in a math class, and in the next room, divided by a curtain, is a history class. If you were to remove the curtain between the two classrooms so that students from both classrooms could see each other and interact, would that alter the foundation of the material the students are learning? Do the curricula automatically change because the curtain is no longer there? Of course not: although the physical rooms change, the curricula stay the same. The only difference is that the math class can see the history class and vice versa.

For the sake of this analogy, the math teacher still knows only how to teach math, and the history teacher knows only how to teach history. Removing the curtain first without revising the curricula will likely confuse everyone in both rooms and make for a noisy and perhaps less productive environment overall.

As activists (assuming you consider yourself an activist), we have to ask ourselves the following question: *If we want to change the world, why do we think we have to make current movements converge?* These movements are already infected with colonial logic, which is in part why there are so many rhetorical wrestling matches surrounding talk about multiple oppressions. We have to get to a point in our politics where we realize that our current social movements are products of the colonial order and they deserve to be critiqued and examined just as intensely as the systems of oppression we are fighting. We are so bound by these movements that I believe there are significant constraints on how we envision solutions—constraints that need to be overcome.

I have found that some activists don't realize they can question the ideological frameworks that guide the movements they are in. I have had to remind audiences during many of the presentations I have given that they don't *have* to couch all of their work in intersectionality theory just because they want to talk about multiple oppressions at the same time. There are many theories you can choose from, and which you can modify and apply in new ways.

Moreover, intersectionality simplifies oppressive systems and ignores the nuances of racism, and I believe that in many instances it has prevented holistic insights about racial struggles from emerging. Before we start adding animal bodies to the matrix of oppressions, let's briefly examine how intersectionality ignores the full scope and size of white supremacist violence against Black bodies. This analysis will also provide an explanation for why I believe many well-intentioned anti-racist activists did not notice deeper, zoological elements to Chris's experiences in *Get Out*.

How Intersectionality Ignores Black Men, and Why That's a Problem

Tommy Curry's scholarship (2016) on race and gender highlights the theoretical limitations of intersectionality when it comes to grappling with Black men's experiences with sexual violence from the white supremacist state. Although intersectionality is supposed to center Black women's experiences with racism and sexism, Curry demonstrates how its erasure of Black men's experiences with white supremacist patriarchy also limits how we understand Black women's struggles. And because we have a limited understanding of "racial" oppression and "gendered" oppression (which we collectively regard as distinct and separate), we do not know how to account for the messiness of Black men's or Black women's experiences in the current social order.

For example, when Black men were victims of "stop-and-frisk" police violence (under stop-and-frisk policies, police could legally search the body of any person they assumed had weapons or contraband) (Coates 2013), our compartmentalized movements reacted accordingly. Activists assumed this was an issue for the *anti-racist movements*, and in so doing we missed the *gendered dimensions* of this racial violence. In a Eurocentric setup, "gender" is associated with white women and "race" is associated with Black men (Lugones 2010, 757). Black women are intrinsically erased (which is why we are constantly trying to connect movements to get visibility) and Black men's experiences with sexual violence are ignored because they are not seen as being able to be sexually violated—they are seen as lacking "gender."

Especially since heterosexual Black men themselves are often framed as the ultimate sexual criminals, speaking to their sexual vulnerabilities in a white supremacist state does not fit the mainstream narrative of their supposed innate predatory natures. Typically, the only time gendered oppression with respect to Black men's experiences is considered is when they are gender-nonconforming or homosexual. Despite the fact that heterosexual men are also victims of racialized sexual violence by the state, an analysis of gender never emerges.

Curry offers another example to support his point about intersectionality failing heterosexual Black men. In 2012, when George Zimmerman murdered seventeen-year-old Trayvon Martin in Sanford, Florida—an act that sparked the Black Lives Matter movement—a familiar pattern emerged in our activist movements in response to the killing. The Black Lives Matter movement chalked Martin's experience up to one-dimensional racist violence alone (Cullors 2018). However, most blogs and news sites failed to highlight how Martin may have been scared that Zimmerman was a rapist.

During Zimmerman's trial, Martin's best friend Rachel Jeantel took the stand to revisit the last phone call she had with Martin before he was gunned down. In her testimony, Rachel stated that during the phone call, she warned Martin about Zimmerman potentially being a sexual predator. However, because Martin was a Black *heterosexual male*, feminists and anti-racists alike didn't politicize or unpack this information further. The gendered dimension of his racial experience was overlooked in favor of a prescriptive, simplistic analysis that fit the contours of our society's regressive preconceived notions.

Unfortunately, the Eurocentric compartmentalization of the world continues to inform current anti-racist movements. We can even think about the general consensus among Black feminists that Black men are a part of the "patriarchy" simply because they are male and possess the capacity to individually harm Black women. Terms like "Black patriarchy" (Brown 2018a) have been increasingly employed to describe Black men and women's interactions without a serious understanding of white supremacist history, which would reveal that Black men are incapable of possessing white patriarchal privileges by virtue of being Black men.

Privilege becomes an empty term we throw at anyone whom we find theoretically inconvenient to deal with. T. Hasan Johnson (2017) discusses the limitations of intersectionality in the entire Black Lives Matter movement:

> [. . .] [T]he Black Lives Matter movement is mostly a group of highly educated Black middle-class women who . . . used intersectionality to justify excluding cis-gendered heterosexual Black men from leadership positions in the organization. I not only argue that this is misandrist and ahistorical in regard to characterizing Black men as sexist, misogynistic, and lacking progressivism since slavery, but that it is disingenuous to exploit Black men's deaths for publicity (highlighting them as martyrs) while silencing those who are actively trying to participate. BLM's characterization of Black men is wholly problematic and can be found in the "About Black Lives Matter" section of their website where they state, "It goes beyond the narrow nationalism . . . keeping straight cis Black

men in the front of the movement while our sisters, queer and trans and disabled folk take up roles in the background or not at all" (http://blacklivesmatter.com/). Here, cis-Black men are only presented as a problem to be confronted, while not being invited to lead in any critical capacity for the sake of prioritizing Black women and LGBT, despite those who're most often dying at the hands of police and vigilantes. Here, we are either martyrs or oppressors, and such is untrue and slanderous to say the least. The takeaway? The only good cis-Black men are those that are either silent or dead. . . .

In framing Black men as the ultimate patriarchal predators, we miss how Black men have been and currently are sexually vulnerable to the state, and how they have even experienced systemic sexual violence at the hands of white women (Curry 2018a). In the current setup, if you were to center Black men and their struggles, you could easily be slapped with the label *hotep*, a term that refers to someone who is a "clueless parody of Afrocentricity . . . or someone who's loudly, conspicuously and obnoxiously pro-Black but anti-progress" (Young 2016).

By contrast, T. Hasan Johnson and Tommy Curry are not trying to decenter Black women and their struggles, but they offer an alternative vision for broaching conversations about white supremacy and patriarchy that takes into account the *full* history of sexual violations against both groups. Centering this history certainly doesn't take away from the reality that Black men harm Black women in domestic violence situations, for example. It simply honors the historical reality of how racism and colonialism have actually manifested themselves as systems of oppression in which sexual violence and racial violence are undeniably intertwined.

Within an intersectional analysis, we tend to miss how Black men were sexually vulnerable during slavery and were routinely raped by white men *and* women. Curry (2018b) writes:

While we are more familiar with the rape of Black women during slavery, the story of Black male rape by white men and women is often overlooked. Not unlike other British colonies, the bodies of male natives were exoticized and often the objects of colonial fetishes (Sen 2010; Aldrich 2003). Black males were raped, mutilated, and eaten during American slavery (Woodard 2014). The bodies of Black men were thought to be potions of virility to whites and were often consumed as a ritual. . . . The rape of Black males during slavery was often exercise[d] as the ultimate demonstration of power and punishment. The mass rape of Black males during slavery was an unbridled show of force that often resulted in death. . . . It was not only white men who committed rape; the white woman was too a rapist. . . . In the institution of slavery, white women had complete control and access to Black male flesh. She was a master, so to speak, and able to determine the Black male slave's life or death. . . . In this world, white women could use Black male slaves for their personal enjoyment without risking their reputations. . . . [O]ur ability to think of Black males as victims of sexual violence throughout history is obscured by our notions of gender and the vulnerability certain bodies are believed to have to rape. (247–8)

Intersectionality doesn't account for the messiness of race and gender and in part also misses how racism *itself* is sexual violence. That is very different from saying race *can* intersect with gender (as separate phenomena). What decolonial scholars argue is that race and gender *constitute one another* rather than intersect, and this produces entirely new analyses that go above and beyond intersectional discourse.

Contemporary intersectional anti-racist movements' framing of Black men as "privileged" is frankly a vulgar statement: that Black men who have been consumed, raped, mutilated, and tortured in the

U.S. throughout history are now magically "privileged" by virtue of possessing penises seems like a mind-numbingly irresponsible and thoughtlessly prescriptive analysis. Additionally, that individual men like R. Kelly, for example, have access to wealth and participate in the routine sexual abuse of Black women and underage girls certainly doesn't mean that on a systemic level, Black men, as a group, have access to *white male privilege*. T. Hasan Johnson (2015) writes:

> [A]ssumptions about Black males as patriarchal are highly problematic in that they assume "patriarchy" as an institution (or set of interlocking institutions) that exist in a static context, in all places for all time to benefit anyone with a penis. This type of lazy analysis has unfairly branded males of all ages across race, class, and most particularly gender in an uncritical, unreflective manner. . . . [D]espite whatever may be in a given culture, Western cultural colonialism imposed patriarchy on its victims—namely African Americans. It is likely that this cultural imposition may have produced *residual benefits . . .* but these are not privileges, nor do these practices encapsulate how Black men see themselves or their roles in families. . . . Let's be clear about something. Privilege is an extension of power. Period. Privilege provides elites with opportunities to segregate those with it from those without it, and if you don't possess the institutional means to create it or maintain it, __*you. don't. have. privilege.*__ This is why I use the notion of *residual benefits*. It's a more useful way of describing what oppressed groups have that appear to be privileges. Residual benefits are crude advantages with the appearance of privilege but lack the institutional backing of privileges (i.e. Black women share in the benefits of feminists' gains, but still suffer intersectionally in a wide variety of ways). They may give the appearance of privilege in

one given regard (male, hetero, or rich), but often for Black men, such intersections often don't mean privilege, but more complex forms of institutional oppression.

If we don't see the full picture of our oppression, then our activism will be missing crucial parts and perspectives, with direct consequences for how we organize for our own liberation. Because this history of Black male sexual vulnerability has been ignored (and oftentimes there is a stigma associated with being male and a victim of sexual violence), and because the history of white women's predatoriness (with respect to their sexual consumption of Black men and women's bodies) has in turn been buried and treated as an inconvenience in many modern-day feminist circles, Black women today are told that linking arms with white women to fight white supremacist patriarchy is the best route to securing their own freedom.

I remember watching the 2017 women's march after Donald Trump was elected president of the United States. Janelle Monae, a Black actress and musician, performed a song called "Say Her Name" to acknowledge the Black women who have been killed by police violence. #SayHerName as a hashtag on Twitter and as an intersectional social movement started in response to the way that the media were ignoring Black women's murders. Black women highlighted how Black men are "privileged" by virtue of the media attention they received for being *murdered*.

Even in a song intentionally about state-sanctioned violence against *Black women*, in which Monae specifically calls out the names of Black women who have been murdered by the state, she *still* includes the names of Black men and boys like Trayvon Martin and Jordan Davis. This demonstrates that the racial caste system that enacts violence upon Black men and Black women is one and the same, and that we should view it as such rather than crudely trying to pretend there is a hard, definitive boundary.

In fact, most of the women of color who were invited to speak on stage at the march spoke mainly about racial violence, whereas the white women predominantly spoke about mainstream popular topics relegated to women, such as the pay gap. This matters. This demonstrates that Black and Brown women are trying to organize with white women when we might actually have more in common with men of color in the fight against white supremacist patriarchal violence. In this instance, one could also argue that intersectionality does not accurately represent Black women's experiences, which are divided along a "race road" and a separate "gender road." That is not how oppression manifests itself in real life. We are not mere fragmented roads that can converge; we are whole to begin with and we need a theoretical framework that accounts for that fact.

Considering that intersectionality does not do a good job of accounting for the messiness of gendered and racial oppression for either Black men or women, I believe we would be mistaken to throw "animal oppression" onto the tangled highway of overlapping oppressions—simply because intersectionality cannot handle all of these oppressions, nor was it originally intended to. In order to have a robust framework for understanding all of these different oppressions, we need a new model that operates outside of "intersections"—outside of misleading, demonstrably inaccurate conceptions of "connections." Only when we have a new model will we be able to see that just as heterosexual Black men's sexual experiences matter in our conversations about gender, for example, animal experiences matter in conversations about race.

Dimensions Instead of Intersections

Learning to Decode the Liberatory Message
When I was young, I watched the film *Contact*, starring Jodie Foster as Eleanor "Ellie" Arroway, a scientist tasked with finding evidence for extraterrestrial life. In an attempt to make contact with an alien life form, Arroway listens to radio emissions from space. Eventually, she gets a signal

from the star system Vega (about twenty-six light years away) consisting of more than 60,000 pages of data that she struggles to decode.

She decides to meet with a math expert, who also happens to be her secret financial benefactor, who informs her that she is reading the message incorrectly. The message from the aliens, who just so happen to be referred to as *Vegans* (pronounced "vey-guhns"), is not two-dimensional, meaning that you can't read it like a message written on a piece of paper.

Their message is three-dimensional.

You essentially have to put all of the sheets of paper together in order to unlock the message, which forms a three-dimensional blueprint. After Arroway reads the three-dimensional images, she discovers that the pages reveal the schematics for a machine that is to be used as a form of transportation for a single individual. Arroway was limited in her search for the solution because she was viewing the problem in a way that prevented her from understanding the true scope and form of the message. Similarly, we as activists are told that white supremacy looks like this . . .

and gender looks like this . . .

. . . and class looks like this.

They thus become two-dimensional, flattened-out structures rather than components of a larger system. We are missing out on effective solutions to our problems in part because we are not *thinking* about the problems properly. Claire Jean Kim (2016) writes: "[G]ender is not an independent category that is analogous and parallel to race, but rather a category that is refracted or lived through race."

In other words, race, as an organizing principle, is multidimensional.

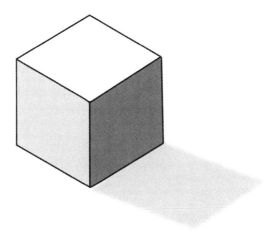

If we were to think of oppression as a literal structure, like a house, this would be the visual difference. According to a two-dimensional understanding of oppression, the oppressive systems look like the illustration on the next page. They all occupy the same space but are disconnected. Each structure represents its own oppression, with its own unique two-dimensional architecture.

By contrast, according to a multidimensional understanding of oppression, the house looks like the illustration below:

Our understanding of a problem will undoubtedly shape how we create solutions to that problem. So if you understand a problem only through a two-dimensional lens, you will see two-dimensional solutions, which aren't solutions that really get to the root of the problem. In that setup, multiple movements will be invoked, each to tackle one oppression, because even in intersectional spaces, each oppression is seen as disconnected from the others. Naturally, if you understand that the issue is multidimensional and composed of other topics and issues, then the solution will be multidimensional as well.

Based on your understanding of white supremacy, you will have different strategies for taking down this structure. For activists who have a two-dimensional understanding of the system, all they see is the front door in the illustration on the previous page and that's their only mode of entrance. They see multiple houses that need to be taken down, so they need to multiply their energy in order to destroy them. In fact, these activists tend to get burned out and exasperated pretty quickly (Gorski 2019), because there is so much ground to cover and so many different structures to get inside of. They may end up pledging their allegiance to only one group to perhaps preserve and focus their energy.

In concrete terms, two-dimensional activists see only the face or surface of the problem, which tends to involve obvious culprits, like individual white people. Two-dimensional anti-racist activists will spend their energy educating white people, fighting them on cultural appropriation, and trying to discipline the ways in which white folks are engaging with the world.

The anti-racist movement isn't the only movement limited by this logic. To fight speciesism as a two-dimensional structure, for example, activists are trained to focus on factory farming and other industries that specifically thrive off of the physical exploitation of animal bodies. In the "gender" house, many feminists more often than not focus on men being the problem and will typically foreground predominantly the experiences of white women in the U.S. In this setup, Black men are seen as a part of the patriarchy as well, so white women and Black women must link arms to take down the structure. They will hold women's marches and large rallies, fighting against those they think are patriarchal. These expressions of two-dimensional activism tend to get the most attention in our mainstream culture because they are easy to spot.

Activists who see white supremacy as a multidimensional structure notice that the house has a side door and a back door as you can see in the illustration on page 90. Multidimensional activists have multiple entrances into the structure, meaning that they don't necessarily just see the obvious way in (the front door). They see that multiple social factors and actors are buttressing structural oppression, which is why they may choose to go around the back and the side, climb in through a skylight, etc.

Multidimensional social theory posits that white supremacy impacts many more than just racialized humans. Animals as well as the environment are a part of this project. There are multiple dimensions of the structure, suggesting that understanding and noticing that such dimensions exist are the first step to bringing down the structure. These activists understand that there are multiple dimensions they have to familiarize themselves with if they want to abolish white supremacy.

Two-dimensional and multidimensional activists share many overlaps in their concerns; however, conflicts have naturally arisen in the past because their ways of actualizing activism can look very different. *Anti-racist animal rights advocates* understand how animality is central to white supremacist logic; however, *two-dimensional anti-racist activists* see us going past the front door in the illustration on the next page (excessive use of force by law enforcement officials and other obvious forms of racism) and assume we've abandoned the cause, whereas we are merely entering through the back door or the skylight. We are approaching liberation from a different, more covert angle.

I also want to note that my articulation of multidimensional theory is not an extension of intersectionality as some might argue (Mutua 2012; 2013). When I started thinking about systems of oppression in terms of dimensions instead of intersections, I was not aware that a rich literature already exists that theorizes about multidimensionality, specifically within the legal studies framework. I have found that even when I state that I use "dimensions" instead of "intersections," some people still think I'm just using another metaphor for an intersection, which is understandable but incorrect.

We are all so chained to the intersectional model, and it has become such a trendy term, that even those of us who are overtly rejecting it in favor of new models still face activists who assume we are operating within the realm of intersectionality. Even some of the early writers on multidimensionality theory subscribe to the idea that "multidimensionality is not a wholly alternative paradigm. Rather it can be seen as drawing upon, extending, and developing intersectionality" (Hutchinson 1997,

641). Although I can see how multidimensionality theory within a legal framework expands on intersectionality, I am not operating within that framework and I do not see multiple dimensions as being in any way similar to intersections. Again, our understanding of the problem has to take a new shape altogether, which will inform our movements for liberation.

Over time, I have realized that the movements *themselves* are unfortunately becoming problematic spaces because some activists are resistant to rethinking the solutions they've created. Our activist setup is a product of the oppressive system we are fighting. Thus I don't support forcibly joining Black Lives Matter and the animal rights movement: that bypasses the important work we need to do to envision new, **afrofuturist** liberatory solutions that have the potential to be more effective than those of popular modern-day social movements.

The reality is that Black scholars and activists have always tried to grapple with animality in Black activism and revolution. This has not necessarily been expressed through veganism or an engagement with veganism, but it presents itself as a unique engagement with the multi-dimensionality of white supremacy. Just as Tommy Curry demonstrates how including Black men's experiences with sexual violence in a racist state will expand our activist horizons, I am arguing that by including animals in our understanding of "race," we will have more robust movements for change.

Che Gossett (2015) similarly points to critical Black radical thinking as an effective intervention for both animal oppression and racial oppression:

> Black people have historically been portrayed through scientific racism as animal like and this anti-black discourse has overlapped with the ways that the animal has been depicted throughout the course of Western philosophy as the desolate ground upon and against which the human, as a colonial and racial construct, has been defined. Yet, Black radical thinkers from Frederick Douglass, to Frantz Fanon and Angela Davis

illustrate how the Black radical tradition offers up—as part of what W. E. B. Du Bois called "the gift of black folk"—a vision of freedom for all life. Black thought provides us with new questions, horizons and meanings for critical animal studies and new pathways for considering abolition as an ongoing aspiration for human-animal-life liberation.

This means that in order to move closer to liberation, we have to both rearticulate our relationship with animals and grapple with the internal effects of the zoologo-racial order on our psyches and liberatory theories. At this juncture, some readers may ask: *Well, what does a multidimensional analysis of racial liberation look like?* The next chapter proposes an answer to this question. Rather than concentrating on the ways in which racial oppression *connects* with animal oppression (intersectional analysis), we will focus on a term I call *afro-zoological resistance*, which demonstrates how white supremacy is *composed* of anti-animal sentiments and that in order to take down this ideology, our activism must include a robust analysis of animals within the racial landscape.

4

Afro-Zoological Resistance

Fighting the Racial Appetite of White Supremacy

John S. Jacobs referred to his former masters as "human fleshmongers" possessed of an unnatural hunger for human flesh and soul.—**Vincent Woodard** (2014, 264)

One of the main ways in which the West has canned the natural in order to consume it has been in the development of public displays of our human power over nature.
—**Reniel Rodríguez Ramos** (2014, 8)

For as long as Africans have been Americans, they have had no entitlement to speak for or about nature.
—**Kimberly Ruffin** (2010, 1)

IN ORDER TO EXPLORE WHAT A MULTIDIMENSIONAL ANALYSIS OF ANTI-racist activism looks like, I want to return to *Get Out* because I think Chris's actions symbolically offer us a glimpse of an afrofuturist activism that centers animality. *Get Out* is powerful not only because it offers, through a form of popular entertainment, a comprehensive look at the inner workings of white supremacist violence that I discussed earlier; it also displays the anatomy of white supremacist zoological witchcraft, whereby "animality" is used to justify the consumption and control of minoritized bodies.

Additionally, *Get Out* offers a symbolic vision for what multidimensional anti-racist activism might look like. As I mentioned earlier, a lot of well-intentioned activists have noticed obvious markers of white supremacy in the film, such as the buck's head on the wall and the white people who lure Black folks into traps. However, running through the film are much deeper themes of afrofuturist afro-zoological resistance.

In *Get Out*, the grammar system for colonialism is consumption—the act of reducing beings to mere flesh to be eaten and/or manipulated. This is how the racial system communicates its power. *Animal* is part of the vocabulary of white supremacist violence; it signifies the rhetorical and social branding of certain bodies, which white supremacy wants to consume, exploit, and eliminate without question. The deer whom Rose hits with her car and the buck's head that hangs from the wall, in addition to the leather chair in the basement, are all part of the racial vocabulary of white supremacy.

If we acknowledge the zoological dimensions of white supremacy, then we can "read" the expressions of animal violence in *Get Out* as part of the racial landscape. In part, "getting out" means familiarizing ourselves with the grammar system of white supremacy so that we can read the full message. Only in so doing can we create a new lexicon that unlocks new potentials and new ways of engaging in resistance and the fight for freedom.

I advocate a form of activism called afro-zoological resistance that centers animality in our understanding of racial liberation. I believe that *Get Out* can serve as a kind of pop culture signpost pointing us in the right direction with regard to how we conceptually engage with notions of animality and race. The question isn't how animal experiences *intersect with* Black experiences in *Get Out*. The question is: *How does white supremacy use both minoritized bodies and animality to communicate and re-inscribe a mythical fantasy of racial superiority?*

How Nature Became the Playground for White Supremacy

Kimberly Smith (2007) writes:

> One might think that 250 years of slavery would have left black Americans permanently alienated from the American landscape. Forced for generations to work the earth without just reward, without the right to own land, without even the

freedom to travel, what meaning could they find in America's pristine wilderness? Locked in a struggle for social justice, what interest could they have in the claims of nature? (1)

In the American imagination, natural spaces are popularly framed as "white" spaces, in part because Black people were not allowed to enter certain parks or outdoor spaces until segregation ended (Meraji 2015). Most Black folks would not take their children into the woods or forests out of fear that something "bad" would happen. The desire to protect oneself and one's family from white supremacist violence translated into a cultural narrative that framed Black folks as being detached from nature. I can't tell you how many times I've encountered stereotypes that advertise the idea that Black folks don't swim, camp, go hiking, travel, etc. These pernicious narratives are so pervasive because the dominant class fears Black people might trust their own sensibilities with the natural world.

Historically, nature has served as a site for some of the most heinous, violent racial crimes ever committed, which was captured by *The Guardian* in an article titled "'Bad Things Happen in the Woods': The Anxiety of Hiking While Black" (Pires 2018). Consequently, "[s]tereotypes persist that African Americans are physically and spiritually detached from the environment. This wrongheaded notion is so engrained in our culture that many of us have begun to believe it ourselves. But nothing could be less true" (Glave 2010, 3). Therefore, nature has become almost the embodiment of white supremacy:

Nature is not merely the material environment. . . . Race and nature are both material and symbolic. . . . Natural character is written into discourse and expressions but is also worked into flesh and landscape. . . . Race provides a critical medium through which ideas of nature operate, even as racialized forces rework the ground of nature itself. (Moore, Kosek, and Pandian 2003, 3)

Diane Glave specifically wrote her book *Rooted in the Earth: Reclaiming the African American Environmental Heritage* (2010) to reclaim narratives about environmentalism often regarded as a "white domain." She provides several examples to showcase how Black folks have always worked *within* nature to actualize their dreams of racial liberation. We can think of Harriet Tubman walking through dense forests and woods to follow the North Star, which guided her and others to freedom. Enslaved Africans seeking liberation knew that moss grew on the north side of trees and learned that birds migrated north:

> Thus, slavery itself forced the slaves . . . out into the uncultivated landscape, and the slaves gained substantial knowledge and experience because of that. . . . [T]hey also acquired the intrinsic understanding of how to interact and co-exist with nature, how to identify and avoid danger, and how to survive. . . . [T]he slaves learned how to maneuver in the uncultivated landscapes undetected." (Turner 2012, 59)

Nature provided its own roadmap for liberation that Black people could follow to freedom:

> Wilderness evoked both fear and comfort for African Americans. The woods, forests, and swamps were natural places where blacks were hunted and mauled or lynched and hung from trees. . . . But the wilderness was also a refuge, a place to live long-term, or a place of transition for runaways between the plantation and freedom. (Glave, 59)

Nature serves as a racial paradox in *Get Out*; it is a site of violence against Black bodies as well as a space for liberation.

During the film's opening credits, the camera quickly pans through images of woods and trees while ominous music plays in the background. Later in the film, the viewer learns that the Armitage home is quietly tucked behind layers of dense forests, re-inscribing colonial tropes of nature as a tool for carrying out and concealing racial violence. Dean Armitage tells Chris: "The nearest house is across the lake . . . it's total privacy." It's not a coincidence that the Armitage home has colonial architecture, conjuring up slave plantation aesthetics. The all-Black staff working as laborers accentuates this theme.

In order to escape from the Armitages' basement after being hypno-tized and bound to the leather chair, Chris makes use of signifiers of nature that are also imbued with racial significance (for example, the cotton and the buck's head) to break free. Cotton in particular is an item that evokes a visceral response from most people who have even basic knowledge of U.S. racial history. Cotton has become an expression of white supremacist consumption—the use and abuse of Black bodies to fuel an economy. Cotton is often conflated with white supremacy itself, which again represents the dominant class's successful attempt at controlling and defining nature through its own power systems.

However, "enslaved people who worked daily in rice fields or with other crops understood the environment better than the slaveholders" (Glave 2010, 85). Cotton should not be seen as a signifier of white supremacist mastery but as an emblem of Black resilience and survival. Without using words, *Get Out* articulates this contradiction when Chris uses cotton as a vehicle to free himself.

To paraphrase Audre Lorde, it's not that the master's tools can't bring down his house, *it's that the master's tools were never his to begin with*. The dominant class manipulated natural spaces, environments, and bodies to serve its own oppressive agenda. Chris rips the chair's leather with his fingers, breaking the fragile dermis of white supremacist domination that is symbolized by transmogrified cow skin. As I noted earlier, the animal elements and skins throughout the home act as emblems of white supremacy's attempts to master nature. Chris acts the way he does almost without intention, as though he's being guided by a kind of hypnotic racial reflex.

It's almost as if Chris has been here before, in this exact scenario, and he knows exactly what to do—a racial déjà vu moment so to speak. Picking cotton, while a marker of Black oppression, simultaneously marks Black survival. This legacy of survival is what guides Chris through his captivity. Many viewers celebrate the moment when Chris rips cotton from the chair he's bound to and stuffs it in his ears to avoid further hypnosis by Missy. Not only is the "cotton moment" a nod to antebellum slavery, animality, and captivity, it also is a commentary on taxidermy and zoological racism. Not only is the taxidermied buck's head stuffed with white racial fantasies and projections, but the cow skin is also transformed into a stuffed item—reshaped to fit the comforts of white supremacy.

I want to note that although Black and Brown communities all over the globe have used and continue to use animal bodies for their own benefit, there is something unique about the ways in which white supremacy foisted a racial system on these practices to bolster white people's own superiority to the rest of the natural world:

> [I]f taxidermy denotes a material practice—the dissection, hollowing out, and restuffing of a corpse's epidermal shell—its connotative specters revive fantasies of white male supremacy in "the sporting crucible" of colonial mastery over nature, and of the conquest of time and mortality through the preservation of the semblance of life in death. In this context, taxidermy functions as a powerful nodal point in a matrix of racial and species discourses, narratives of disappearance and extinction, and tropes of aboriginality that have been crucial to the maintenance of colonial power. . . . (Wakeham 2008, 5–6)

All of the bodies used by the white people in *Get Out* are transformed into vehicles that serve the dominant class. Chris uses the cotton as an armor to defend himself against being turned into another piece of zoological furniture. He stuffs his ears to prevent being "stuffed" with white projections.

At the same time that he uses the cotton as a vehicle to liberate his mind, Chris also makes use of the bust of the taxidermied buck on the wall to help him take down the oppressor, embodied by Rose's father. Thus, he *closes the distance* between his body and the animal—a strategy that is not usually employed in our anti-racist movements. Chris removes the bust of the buck from the wall and charges at Dean, driving the antlers into his neck. Although one could argue that the buck is already deceased and that like Dean, Chris is using the animal's corpse for his own gain, his use of the buck is both a form of symbolic revenge and an overt reclamation of the animal as an emblem of nature as well as a stereotype of Black men.

In this instance, Chris is weaponizing animality. It's important that we have a symbolic reading of this scene. Obviously, Peele is not advertising the literal killing of white people as a means of achieving racial empowerment; however, I see an explicit nod to the reclamation of animality in our efforts to dismantle the system (Ko & Ko 2017, 63).

Chris shows us that we need to abandon our former choreography of resistance, which relies upon stepping on the animal, and instead move our bodies closer together for true liberation. In reference to historical Black activism and animality, Lindgren Johnson (2018) writes:

The focus, for example, is not on how African Americans shake off animal associations in demanding recognition of their humanity, but on how they hold fast to animality and animals in making such a move, revising "the human" itself as they go and undermining the binaries that helped to produce racial and animal injustices.

Again, I would refer to this as afro-zoological resistance, which I assert is the bedrock of true anti-racist activism. We can't free ourselves from the dominant power structure if we can't locate or even imagine breaking free of its zoological roots. This requires us, as people of color, to not only note the ways in which we are "animalized" by the dominant system but also reconsider our own attitudes and behaviors toward literal animals. Revising our understanding of white supremacy through a zoological filter opens up activist possibilities for minoritized people to work alongside/for nonhuman animals.

Afro-zoological elements are woven throughout *Get Out*. After Chris kills Dean, who falls and knocks over one of the candles in the surgical room, he throws the taxidermied buck's head on the ground, symbolizing the end of white supremacist power.[1] After he does this, a fire starts and inevitably spreads throughout the entire home. *Get Out* represents a mediated shift toward envisioning afro-zoological rebellion *as* anti-racist activism, and it exemplifies a burgeoning genre of media[2] that depicts Black people as internally healed from double consciousness when they explicitly confront the zoologo-racial order that keeps white supremacy intact.

White Supremacist Manipulation of Natural Senses

This leads us to a secondary, perhaps even more metaphorical analysis of *Get Out* and afro-zoological resistance—an analysis that points to double consciousness. Not only does white supremacy attempt to manipulate natural spaces, lands, and bodies in order to naturalize its superiority, it also tries to manipulate the natural senses of the oppressed. White supremacy attempts to convince minoritized subjects that the universe is its domain just as it attempts to get "inside" and reside within our consciousnesses.

The Armitages want to consume Chris's soul and/or consciousness, and use an almost ritualized form of racial hypnosis to submerge Chris in the sunken place. As I've argued earlier, the sunken place exists in the bellies of white supremacist fantasies, where it ingests Black souls much like a shamanistic practitioner eats the soul of an enemy:

> Where indigenous practice of witchcraft is understood to involve the consumption of "dead" flesh, the slavery of early modernity opens a new "after-death" prospect: the *zombi* state, the living cannibalization of commercial capital, flesh not so much as food for thought as gold for trade. (Perkinson 2004, 623)

Part of the shamanistic power of white supremacy is its ability to strip us of our natural senses. This is why the sunken place, where Chris is stripped of agency and becomes a passenger rather than the operator of his own body, is purposely set in Black space. Our sensibilities are stripped from us; this is significant because we all use our senses to gather information about and to make sense of our environments. Black people's consciousnesses become disoriented beings floating in this space—in the void; our bodies become extensions of whiteness or white appendages. The white people who have their brains transplanted into Black bodies control the bodies' functions. Their observations and their senses overpower our own. In fact, the white "owners" even rename the Black bodies in an attempt to flex their social and racial power. We never learn the actual identity of "Georgina" or "Walter." This renaming ritual is a crucial component of historical enslavement and white cannibalism. Renaming and redefining are necessary steps in ingesting someone's land, culture, body, and consciousness.

Throughout the film, Chris expresses uneasiness around the Black staff and even shares his discomfort with Rose, who routinely denies or minimizes his observations. He is disciplined into trusting her observations and her version of events—the first phase of the fracturing of his consciousness. This is how racism operates: it's an everyday ritual that slowly chips away at the confidence of the oppressed, in order to ensure that we trust the sensibilities of the dominant class. We become convinced that we are living in *their* world.

Rose prepares Chris's flesh for consumption by slowly consuming his mind. She grooms him into doubting himself, which makes him trusting enough to sit with Rose's mother and share his inner vulnerabilities. It's not a coincidence that during the hypnosis, Missy asks him very intimate questions related to his faculties, such as what he was watching and what he physically heard outside when his mother passed away.

The sunken place becomes a physical manifestation of the wretchedness of double consciousness; it is where we become paralyzed passengers in our bodies and where our souls are metabolized by the dominant class. Peele visually demonstrates the brutality of double consciousness using the scars on the heads of Black victims who underwent the coagula surgery. Afro-zoological resistance involves not only relocating the animal within the landscape of white supremacist domination but also learning to reclaim our senses and our experiences with nature as well as our natural selves.

When Chris is bound to the leather chair in the basement, he starts picking out the cotton from the chair, which allows for a shift of the ancestral role from slave to liberator. Despite the fact that the Armitages are trying to permanently submerge Chris in the sunken place, Black ancestral whisperings are louder than their hypnotic attempts to get into his head. Thus, signifiers of "colonial mastery" such as cotton and taxidermy become tools used by Chris to subvert the power dynamic he's forced into.

In other words, there appears to be a porous, intergenerational, corporeal wisdom that links slavery to the present. The past is connected to the future, and Chris exhibits how this ancestral whispering can empower the next generation. It's no surprise then that director Jordan Peele chose "Sikiliza Kwa Wahenga," which translates to "listen to your ancestors" in Swahili, as the opening song in *Get Out*. The song's lyrics include "Run! You need to run far! Listen to the truth! Brother, listen to your ancestors! Run! Run! To save yourself, listen to the ancestors" (Gayo 2017). The phrase *sikiliza kwa wahenga* is also whispered at specific moments throughout the film to warn Chris that something is wrong. The song is a nod to the process of healing double consciousness: the ancestral whisperings try to drown out the colonized voice in Chris's head that is keeping him at the Armitages':

> There is often an unspoken understanding within the Black community that is informed by an omnipresent collective memory and this song speaks to that very notion. There is a keen awareness that influences how Black people not only navigate macro systems (institutions of education, criminal justice, etc.), but also small interactions (not-so-micro fucking aggressions). The voices in the song are the voices we carry—the history books we read, or the elders in our communities or the countless videos of police brutality that serve as haunting reminders to stay awake and attuned to the ways white supremacy reinvents itself every day. (Gayo 2017)

The song is also significant because it points to a larger theme in the film: *that white supremacy has socialized Black people to not trust each other's observations either*. "'Get Out' is a fundamentally lonely movie, not merely for what it says about what might lurk behind awkward white attempts at ingratiation, but in the ways the Armitages' nefarious plot divides black people from each other, too" (Rosenberg 2017). Rod Williams, the TSA agent, constantly warns Chris about the Armitages, yet Chris ignores his warnings. Rod also goes to the police to inform them of his own hypothesis about the Armitages' hypnotizing of Black folks, and all of the police (who are people of color) overtly laugh in his face.

When Chris tells Georgina that he feels nervous around the white people, she repeatedly states "no" and adds: "Aren't you something? That's not my experience. . . . [T]he Armitages are so good to us. They treat us like family." *Get Out* demonstrates how white supremacy has fractured Black people's internal consciousnesses as well as our private sites for resistance and movement-building.

Chris's camera becomes a significant artifact in the quest to fight double consciousness as well. As I mentioned in Chapter 2, the flash from his camera is what "wakes" Andre up from his sleepwalking state. Andre tells Chris to "get out." Many other thinkers and writers have noted the significance of the camera today in the Black Lives Matter era, in which the truth oftentimes can be told only through the Black person's lens. The camera becomes a technology of Black truth and racial resistance.

I see the camera as a metaphorical nod to the process of healing double consciousness and trusting our own voices and observations. When we use our *own* lenses, we have the power to heal and wake each other up:

> In many ways, Chris's camera is a mechanical extension of his own eyes . . . over the other bodily senses, vision has long been the most intuitive metaphor for discussing subjective experience. Just as the sense of touch is often evoked to discuss compassion or empathy ("I feel you"), vision is closely linked to a person's unique way of *knowing* the world. (Cruz 2017)

Perhaps it's not surprising then that at every turn, Georgina unplugs Chris's phone in his room when he tries to charge it. Just as Missy attempts to strip Chris's consciousness from his body, Georgina tries to separate Chris from his technology of racialized resistance—the one lens that confirms his reality.

In this sense, freedom for Black folks means drowning out the internal voice of our oppressor and reclaiming the elements of our natural selves that once were (and unfortunately still are) seen as the colonizer's property. There is a reason why those in the dominant class are constantly attempting to fracture our consciousnesses: there is power in trusting your own sensibilities. Only when Chris realizes that he is going to share the same fate as Georgina, Walter, Andre, and the taxidermied buck does he start listening to his own voice and the whisperings of his ancestors. He starts to trust his lens, which guides him to plug his ears with the cotton and to see how the bust of the buck can help him take down his captors. All of the racial signposts Chris initially ignored become emblems of his liberation. Once he trusts his own lens and his own perspective, the blueprint for escape emerges.

Anti-racist activists must come to the conclusion that white supremacy is a zoological structure that relies upon the manipulation of nature and of the senses of the oppressed, as well as the harming of animals as part of its own fantasies of superiority. This means that we as anti-racist activists must go *through*—not around—animals to actualize our own liberation. Animals are a part of the grammar of white supremacist violence. To combat this cannibalistic system and force, we must reject the colonial order that has been foisted on us and that strips us of our natural senses as well as our rightful space in the world. Most importantly, we have to reclaim our voices and our perspectives—which we are constantly denied ownership of.

5

FREEING THE ANIMAL
FROM THE GRASP
OF THE ANIMAL RIGHTS MOVEMENT

Final Thoughts

A shift in the valuation of animals, if it is to be transformative and not merely a reallocation of attribution within a racially hierarchical system of value, must be accompanied by a different mode of political social life and grammar of representation.—**Zakiyyah Iman Jackson** (2016)

My observations of and participation in settler animal advocacy movements in North America have left me cynical that meaningful change can be affected for nonhuman animals without situating both animal enterprise and the animal liberation movement in the context of the settler colonial state. —**Justin Kay** (2019)

*I*F ANTI-RACIST MOVEMENTS PROPERLY LOCATE THE ZOOLOGICAL DIMENSIONS OF *white supremacist violence, then animals have a chance of being set free thanks to multidimensional anti-racist organizing efforts. So how does the contemporary animal rights movement fit into this conversation?*

The animal rights movement has largely ignored scholarship from anti-racist activists who have meaningful things to say about white supremacy's appetite for flesh and power. Minoritized people's experiences with white colonialist, cannibalistic violence have been framed as irrelevant to animal experiences, despite the fact that minoritized subjects have been forced to walk on a human–animal tightrope for generations. Interrogating animality has always been within the domain of most human movements and human rights struggles, particularly racial struggles. However, the fight for animals has still historically been framed largely as a "white-centered" movement.

How did this happen? How has the rich tradition of racial scholar-ship centered on the human/animal binary become disconnected from the mainstream animal rights movement? Interactions with animals are unquestionably seen as falling within the domain of white society, from hunting and taxidermy to fighting for their rights. The only way that Black and Brown people can participate is seemingly through a narrative of "diversity," not epistemology.

The animal rights movement swallows up and digests whole histo-ries of animal advocacy that existed before the term *vegan* was even coined. This isn't just about the fact that advocacy by people of color has been ignored and intellectually gentrified, but the Eurocentric animal rights movement has completely paved over other ways of thinking about animals and of approaching animal advocacy. This is in part why a lot of animal rights activists (even activists of color) aren't familiar with the rich history and tradition of Black people interrogating animality in their own movements for liberation.

The animal rights movement has a substantial amount of funding available. However, most financial resources are distributed to activists who predominantly focus on *physical* animal oppression. They are seen as *directly* helping animals. Unfortunately, by contrast, those of us who grapple with animal oppression in *indirect* ways, by confronting racialized power systems (Johnson 2018), are seen as distracting and are not given the resources we need to tackle the structures that hurt both animals and ourselves. One might even ask: If anti-racist activists acknowledge the human–animal tightrope as central to racism (which then allows us to find suitable ways to tackle animal oppression), is a standalone animal rights movement even necessary?

This is a controversial question. My goal in asking this isn't to dismiss the power of the animal rights movement, nor am I advocating that one movement *alone* fix all of the issues. I have met animal rights activists who work tirelessly for the freedom of animals and spend every waking hour doing what they can to alleviate their suffering. I am not attempting to minimize these efforts or ignore the advances the movement has made toward liberating animals.

However, I can't help but wonder if there might be more effective ways of freeing animals that simultaneously bring animal oppression into conversation with other oppressions from the *beginning* (without relying upon intersectional theory whereby the "connection" often happens too late in the game). Since most animal rights activists cling to veganism as the dominant vehicle to relieve the suffering of animals, many vegans assume that by giving up meat they've achieved some nirvana and now it's their job to teach others to do the same.

As I suggested at the beginning of this book, anchoring complex conversations about animality and race to kale and vegan burgers bypasses the point. Throughout this book, I have attempted to demonstrate just how complex these conversations can be, especially when we reframe animal experiences using a racial lens.

It's easy to scoff at members of the public who "don't get" animal rights or don't see the contradictions in their own behaviors (for example, that they love dogs but eat cows). However, I see almost everyone I meet as a potential animal rights activist; it's just that the dominant modes of activism and the theories structuring our movements have completely turned them off from ever exploring these concepts further. It is important to note that being critical of mainstream animal rights *activism* does not automatically equate to being a proponent of animal oppression.

Many animal rights activists often frame critics of the animal rights movement as uncompassionate or cruel, rather than being reflective and pointing the finger at their own movements and theories. This is why I think it's important that we offer alternative frameworks outside of veganism and anti-speciesism for talking about animals.

In fact, sometimes in my talks I try to politically motivate people to not eat meat by appealing to racialized frameworks that demonstrate the zoological nature of white supremacy. This isn't to say that I am ashamed of being vegan. I loudly and proudly claim the *vegan* label when I meet people to demonstrate that there is nothing embarrassing about this lifestyle. Nonetheless, I have come to the conclusion that the *animal rights/vegan movement is not the only movement that advocates on behalf of animals.* In fact, I feel that some intellectual and activist spaces outside of the animal rights movement tend to create better theory about animal oppression.

This is why I have found that categorized thinking and social movement identity are hurting our liberation movements. If you don't describe yourself as an animal rights activist or a vegan, people assume that your ideas are not relevant to their quest to free animals. However, we need to encourage people to read across disciplines so they realize that others who seemingly have absolutely nothing to do with their goals could provide them with new concepts and ideologies that are central to solving their problems.

Veganism (as a diet) is merely a natural byproduct of a larger conceptual shift—it's not the main point. Let's draw a parallel with the natural hair movement, which focuses on dismantling Eurocentric beauty standards in the Black community.

Growing up, I absolutely hated my natural hair texture. I would have dreams in which I had straight long hair running down my back (in addition to green or blue eyes). When I woke up, I would cry after realizing the straight long hair I had dreamed about was actually a frizzy afro on top of my head. When I was in elementary school, I asked my mother if she could start using toxic straightening chemicals, referred to as "relaxers," in my hair. These kits are sold in beauty salons around the country as well as in everyday grocery stores. Relaxer companies also create kits for children. Just as McDonald's offers Happy Meals with toys in the packages, relaxer kits for children are brightly colored and often come with surprises inside, like music cassettes. Growing up, I used the JUST FOR ME brand by Soft and Beautiful religiously. I learned at a young age that having "relaxed," "tame," "unfrizzy" hair meant I would be considered "soft" and "beautiful."

I chemically straightened my hair for over a decade until I was twenty years old. My hair actually started to fall out. Nonetheless, I still used the chemicals because I didn't actually know how to style my real, natural hair. I was familiar only with a straight texture. When I was twenty, someone introduced me to bell hooks's essay "Straightening Our Hair" (1989), in which she contextualizes Black women's desire for straight hair by highlighting the white supremacist, Eurocentric beauty standards guiding our culture at large.[1] Only when I read this essay did I start to politicize my practices.

I realized that Black women were only given visibility in the media if they had straight hair. Straight hair was equated with professionalism, beauty, and power. It wasn't until I connected those dots that I realized that my everyday habit of "relaxing" my hair was actually guided by a larger, racist framework that decreed natural hair was unruly, undesirable, and untamed, making me terrified to embrace my natural body. I shaved off all of my relaxed hair and started to grow my natural hair. I had not felt my real hair texture in over a decade and had to relearn how to style it.

The moral of the story is that the natural hair movement isn't about hair *per se*—it's a movement seeking to reject Eurocentric standards of beauty and Eurocentric ways of thinking and being. It's not just about going from straight to curly hair. Hair texture is an expression of something much larger. So, for example, it was not a coincidence that when I shaved off all of my relaxed hair, I simultaneously started reading critical race theory and taking classes in African American literature. My transformation did not begin and end with my hair. Hair was just the symptom of something much larger.

Similarly, veganism isn't just about kicking a meat-eating habit and getting some veggies into your diet. It's a powerful rejection of a racist food system and a racist, cannibalistic politics that characterizes animals and nonwhite people as disposable and consumable. This is why anti-racist theory matters in our efforts to free animals. The goal isn't just to get people to replace chicken with tofu (although that's a great start). The goal is to get the public to understand why animals matter on a political and ethical level. The goal is to reveal how the current power structure relies upon anti-Black and anti-animal ideologies to strengthen itself.

The animal rights movement has hitherto claimed ownership of "the animal." Because of the disciplinary arrangement that instructs us to base our understanding of oppression on categorical liberation movements, a lot of people assume that discussing "the animal," both

physically and conceptually, is something for "animal rights activists."
However, this project affects us all; it doesn't matter what movement
you're in. In order for our planet to be sustainable, peaceful, and just, we
have to rid ourselves of these colonial thoughts. We can't move forward
until the animal is free. This is in part why we must conclude that the
animal rights movement doesn't own "the animal."

The reality is that animal oppression is a messy topic when the
animal rights movement treats it as though it's not. When you join
the movement, you are handed an ideological gift box that contains
the book *Animal Liberation*, the term *speciesism*, and the movie *Earthlings*,
among other documentaries such as *What the Health*, *Cowspiracy*, etc. You
are already told how to think about animal oppression and animal
liberation, *and that's the first problem*. These ideological items are treated
like elements of the conceptual uniform you should wear when going
into battle to fight for animals. In reality, this suit of conceptual armor
has a lot of holes in it.

The epistemic anchor of the movement is already Eurocentric and locked; it conveniently leaves out any critical race perspective on animality and animal oppression. This means that people of color can contribute only through the depoliticized lens of diversity rather than through epistemology. *Imagine the perspectives we are missing out on when we think of Blackness only as a diversity strategy rather than a framework to use to rethink animal liberation.*

Lindgren Johnson (2018) writes:

> I am thinking about those authors who practice critical animality studies from *within* and not from without animality and who engage with discourses of animality in ways that open up the current fields of both animal and animality studies today. These visionary thinkers within the black community enact other ways of being human that exceed the assumptions of animality studies and, more broadly speaking, liberal humanism: they begin, in many ways, at the juncture that animality studies asks scholars to stop. (12)

The animal rights movement is largely disconnected from this type of scholarship, which prevents activists from finding viable solutions to the problems they are committed to solving. I'm always amazed by how many people who are new to the animal rights movement start using the term *speciesism*. It makes me wonder: *Why are you using that term?*

Speciesism theory has become almost a religious doctrine in the animal rights movement. Liberation movements are supposed to be messy spaces where people can offer new ways of thinking and doing. However, today you have to know the right language, say all the right things, and extend the knowledge that's already present. Even the intersectional turn within the animal rights movement doesn't necessarily produce new insights about animals, considering that activists just add speciesism to the matrix of oppressions without realizing that they can question speciesism itself as a concept.[2] If we don't have the freedom in our liberation movements to think new thoughts and be messy, what type of liberated world are we actually fighting for at the end of the day?

If you deviate from mainstream ways of talking about animals (usually anchored to conversations about factory farming and speciesism), you're seen as a distraction from the movement; this is a shame considering that "speciesism" was an idea invented by one person. We can see how much of an impact this one idea has had on our culture and on animal protection movements. Imagine if we were as willing to accept other ideas and if we were to implement them as enthusiastically! Speciesism is just one way of looking at the problem. We need new epistemologies and new thought paradigms to lead us forward.

When I was in graduate school, I had a conversation with my professor about the "waves" of the feminist movement. I remember trying to ground my work and thoughts about Black women's experiences in that feminist structure. My professor sent me an article stating that the "waves" model is inherently white because it is based on white women's activism. This is in part why the first wave of feminism began with Susan B. Anthony's efforts. For the first time, I realized that I'd never even thought it a possibility that I could question that setup. *I implicitly assumed I had to work within it.*

There's nothing inherently wrong with celebrating the achievements of white women. That said, there's also nothing inherently wrong with offering an entirely different model for tracking women's activism that decenters Susan B. Anthony and Gloria Steinem. When I gave myself permission to do whatever I wanted to do, the conceptual barriers and compartments blocking my imagination went away. I could think about Black women's futures without having to wrestle with the white "waves" model. Similarly, you don't have to even label yourself a *vegan* or *animal rights activist* to fight for animal liberation. The label *vegan* tracks a particular historical legacy of animal activism and you do not have to adopt this term if you choose to not eat animal bodies and/or if you choose to fight animal oppression.

Our activist movements don't encourage us to think outside the box—outside of the dominant theories and models. These movements have become sites of theoretical purity, where you must subscribe to the dominant modes of thinking or you are seen as impure or heretical (Lee 2017).

Theory matters. Thinking matters. Theorists create the blueprints that guide our movements. If we don't understand how vast animal activism can be and how different it can look from one activist to another, we might be missing opportunities to support projects that, while they appear to have nothing to do with animal rights, are actually contributing to animal liberation. In my talks, I tell audiences that social theory is not always as glamorous as physical activism; however, it is just as necessary.

I like to draw the parallel between the impact of social theory and the impact of an abstract mathematical theory developed in the 1970s called fractal geometry. Fractals are patterns that repeat themselves in a feedback loop.

To most, the theory at first seemed abstract and irrelevant. However, it allowed us to create tiny internal antennae that revolutionized the construction of phones and made cell phones a reality. Smart phones wouldn't exist without fractals.

Mathematicians often create the conceptual foundation for engineers and hands-on people, who make sense of these concepts and apply them to people's everyday, practical needs. Similarly, social theorists create ideas that can then be utilized by activists and thinkers who can make practical sense of what we're saying. Our work is just as necessary as that of the urban farmer, the animal rights activist, and the food justice activist. Thinking and theorizing about animals and race are essential components of the larger project of liberation for all.

I am confident that one day animals will be set free, both literally and conceptually, and I am confident that this will happen with the direction of decolonial Black epistemic frameworks. As Claire Jean Kim (2016) argues: "For animal studies, and feminist studies too, the path forward goes through, not around, black studies." Animal liberation will be achieved in tandem with racial liberation, so long as we understand the multidimensionality of white supremacy.

White supremacy is a brutal and variegated system that has literally and figuratively consumed the bodies and essences of those they see as "animal." We need to wake up from this shamanistic racial trance and listen to the thinkers and theorists who are providing us with the blueprints for getting out. For too long, there has been an attempt not only to physically exploit those who are deemed "animal" but also to submerge the collective psyche in some version of the sunken place. Shedding several hundred years of submergence in religious, political, and corporatized anti-Blackness is no small task. Unfortunately, we may all be (in one form or another) residents of the sunken domain. I hope this book serves as a small light to bring us closer to getting out.

NOTES

Notes Before Reading this Book

1. Many activists and scholars today argue that people of color are reclaiming witchcraft as a practice for healing and coping with oppression. *The Atlantic* published an article on November 5, 2018 titled "The Witches of Baltimore," where Sigal Samuel interviews Black women who left Christianity to embrace African Witchcraft (see Samuel 2018). In the article, Samuel shares that there is an annual Black Witch Convention in the United States. *Wear Your Voice* magazine, an online intersectional feminist digital space, routinely spotlights witches of color, which it did with those who gathered in Washington, D.C. on the anniversary of the 2017 Inauguration of Donald Trump. (See *Wear Your Voice* 2017.)

Introduction

1. Check out the work of lauren Ornelas of Food Empowerment Project and Brenda Sanders of Afro-Vegan Society/Vegan SoulFest. Both are vegan food-justice activists of color who sensitively introduce issues relating to veganism and animal rights to audiences and populations who are experiencing systemic violence themselves.

2. Professor Laura Wright says something similar in her article titled "Introducing Vegan Studies" (see Wright 2018). She states: "Vegan studies constitute a lived and embodied ethic that impacts one's scholarly trajectory; for vegans in the academy, veganism finds its way, via our theoretical musings, into the scholarship that we produce. . . . This field of inquiry is the place toward which I began heading when I was thirteen and visited a sausage plant on a class trip, so I have been living vegan theory for most of my life, even if I didn't realize that that's what I was doing . . . " (8).

3. I am aware how topics relating to food are often ripe with political inquiry. However, on a mainstream level, most folks are not socialized to question their plates or the agricultural industry. This is, in part, why most stories in food sections of newspapers or magazines are filled with recipes or news about restaurants.

4. I am not suggesting that people who commit acts of mass violence are not struggling with mental health issues. Oftentimes they are. I am speaking to how the media immediately frame white or white-passing men as being mentally ill, without a deeper exploration of the ways in which they are ultra-conformists to particular white, violent, masculine identities.

5. I would urge people to read Crenshaw's original document (see Crenshaw 1989), where intersectionality is discussed in context. I would also urge people to watch Kat Blaque's video about intersectionality on YouTube (see Blaque 2018), which provides a comprehensive overview of the intersectional framework. Intersectionality has largely been de-contextualized and used as a framework to discuss the intersections among *all* oppressions. That is how intersectionality is largely understood today, so in my critiques of it, please understand that I am not necessarily examining intersectionality through a legal lens (its original context), but through the larger cultural framework in which it has become a synonym for any connection between any and all oppressions.

6. Syl and I discuss the term *undisciplinary* in an essay we contributed to an anthology on women of color and academia. We held a kitchen-table style conversation where we interviewed each other about our experiences in graduate school, as well as our decisions to leave academia (see Ko & Ko 2019).

7. Tommy Curry discusses this further in his lecture, which you can find on YouTube (see Curry 2018a). He complicates our contemporary understanding of social terms like *gender* and *race*. Activists tend to retroactively apply their modern-day definitions of concepts to history: for example, because we understand white women as experiencing gender oppression today, we assume that white women have *always* dealt with this. Curry argues, however, that historically there was no term to describe gender oppression for white women. They were not even considered to be "minorities."

8. Moya Bailey coined the term *misogynoir*, which is defined as anti-Black misogyny (see Bailey 2018).

1: Anti-Racism vs. Animal Liberation

1. There are, of course, many Black and Brown vegans who specifically center animals in their activism. However, in my experience, I have noticed that plant-based eating and wellness/health seem to dominate these racial spaces.

2. I am not trying to dismiss the importance of wellness conversations in Black spaces, especially because health is so intimately connected to one's political experiences in dominant power structures. As many activists have pointed out, health for people of color *is* a political conversation (see McQuirter 2016). Unfortunately, not a lot of activists are working to connect these political health conversations to animal rights and animality. I think that if these bridges were created, the activism would be even more powerful. I do understand that people enter veganism for a plethora of reasons and often those reasons change and evolve over time, so again, I am not dismissing the power of health and wellness conversations.

3. If you read *Aphro-ism*, you will see how I reference speciesism throughout the text. In my intellectual career, I have always been very open to learning and growing, and often that manifests itself through subscribing to new frameworks while unsubscribing from others.

4. I have to comment on my website Black Vegans Rock (BVR). One could easily look at the website I created and accuse me of doing this very thing—trying to recruit Black people into the mainstream vegan movement. However, that is not the goal of BVR. First of all, I set up the website because a) people kept stating that veganism was a white thing, which was erasing a lot of vegans of color, and b) people of color kept announcing that Black folks weren't vegan, so I made the website to dismiss that claim. BVR is a space where we highlight people who are *already* vegan, rather than try to recruit people into a particular movement or activist space.

5. See Curry 2018a. His lecture addresses the myth that all of women's empowerment is "feminist."

2: White Supremacy as Zoological Witchcraft

1. There is another show in *The Bachelor* franchise world called *Bachelor in Paradise*. Contestants who were eliminated get another chance to compete for love at a resort in Mexico. *Bachelor in Paradise* has a slightly comedic introduction, in which each cast member is featured engaging in an activity they

are "known" for in the franchise. During Season 5, Kendall was featured in the introduction holding an animal skull.

2. I am not trying to appropriate Black struggles here by including nonhuman animals within the definition of racial necrophilia. I am arguing that animals are racialized. Syl Ko (2017) writes:

> Lots of people might laugh if one were to say that eating meat/eggs/ dairy or going to be entertained/learn at the zoo is racist. But that's because race and racism have been framed as phenomena linked only to skin color, the body, or geo-specificity. Race encompasses much more than our limited discourse allows. Race is broad. Race is vague. It hovers over and infects every aspect of our lives, whether we notice it or not. Not only are people and groups raced, but so are regions, so are all members of the environment, so is knowledge, so is language, so is time and space itself. Some might think I'm exaggerating when I say this. They say, "Oh, you just want to make everything about race." Not quite. What I am saying is that race is about everything. (xviii)

3. The act of rendering Black bodies into epidermal shells reminds me a lot of the "cosmetic diversity" of progressive social movements, whereby Black bodies are made to be visible but Black ideas are not invited. Syl Ko (2017) writes: "In short, diversity . . . is the idea that black (and brown) people should function as vessels for white perspectives and white theory as opposed to contributing their own viewpoints and theories. . . . '[D]iversity' is the presence of black bodies, as opposed to the presences of black ideas born from black perspectives in predominantly white spaces" (4).

4. I am aware that Jordan Peele specifically featured an Asian man interested in purchasing a Black body. Ranier Maningding (2017) writes: "By adding one solitary Asian character, Peele highlights the fact that even though

Asians are outnumbered by Black folks, we still take on the role as oppressors by standing on the side of white supremacy and anti-Blackness."

5. Although the material on the chair is never announced, it is assumed to be leather. I have read multiple takes of the film that refer to it as a "leather chair" (see Lang 2018, and Nduaguba 2017).

6. I see *Get Out*'s hyper-representation of colonized Black bodies (suffering from double consciousness) in white spaces as another commentary on cosmetic diversity. I'm reminded of Steve Biko's powerful quote on pseudo-integration in activist spaces:

[T]he integration so achieved is a one-way course, with the whites doing all the talking and the blacks the listening. Let me hasten to say that I am not claiming that segregation is necessarily the natural order; however, given the facts of the situation where a group experiences privilege at the expense of others, then it becomes obvious that a hastily arranged integration cannot be the solution to the problem. It is rather like expecting the slave to work together with the slave-master's son to remove all the conditions leading to the former's enslavement. . . . At the heart of true integration is the provision for each man, each group to rise and attain the envisioned self. Each group must be able to attain its style of existence without encroaching on or being thwarted by another. Out of this mutual respect for each other and complete freedom of self-determination there will obviously arise a genuine fusion of the life-styles of the various groups. This is true integration. From this it becomes clear that as long as blacks are suffering from inferiority complex—a result of 300 years of deliberate oppression, denigration and derision—they will be useless as co-architects of a normal society where man is nothing else but man for his own sake. Hence what is necessary as a prelude to anything else that may come is a very strong grass-roots build-up of black consciousness such that blacks can learn to assert themselves and stake their rightful claim. (Cherry Bomb 2015)

3: Moving from Intersectionality to Multidimensional Liberation Theory

I. *Social justice warrior* is a term born out of the digital sphere that refers to the way that liberals are seen as being "warriors" of justice. It is a term used to humiliate activists who seek to dismantle systems of oppression.

4: Afro-Zoological Resistance

I. Unless white people are literally trying to cut your brain out or otherwise cause you bodily harm, stabbing them indiscriminately is not what I am advocating.

2. *Get Out* certainly isn't the only text that showcases how nature can be used to subvert the racial power dynamic. The episode "Black Museum" (Season 4, Episode 6) of the popular Netflix show *Black Mirror* has a similar ending, in which Nish sets the Black Museum on fire after tricking the racial villain (who also uses technology to oppress Black folks) into drinking poisoned water. The only thing she grabs from the museum before it burns down is a stuffed monkey, yet another commentary on animality and metaphorical consumption.

5: Freeing the Animal from the Grasp of the Animal Rights Movement

I. I don't necessarily agree with everything hooks says in her essay, considering straight hair doesn't always equate to being "brainwashed" by white supremacy. Black women's hair care practices are complex, and the charge of trying to emulate Eurocentric standards of beauty can often be one-dimensional and shallow. I am not opposed to straightening my hair. I had to learn how to see straight hair as a hairstyle rather than a lifestyle.

2. I notice that a lot of vegan activists of color assume they are decentering whiteness by creating racially homogenous spaces that exclude white folks. However, I find that these activists still subscribe to Eurocentric theories such as speciesism.

REFERENCES

Adams, Carol J. 1990. *The Sexual Politics of Meat: A Feminist-Vegetarian Critical Theory*. New York: Continuum.

Aldrich, Richard. 2003. *Colonialism and Homosexuality*. New York: Routledge.

Aloi, Giovanni. 2018. *Speculative Taxidermy: Natural History, Animal Surfaces, and Art in the Anthropocene*. New York: Columbia University Press. (Aloi quotes Rachel Poliquin's *The Breathless Zoo: Taxidermy and the Cultures of Longing*. University Park: Penn State University Press, 2012, 96).

Ansley, Frances. 1989. "Stirring the Ashes: Race, Class and the Future of Civil Rights Scholarship," *Cornell Law Review* 74, no. 6: 993–1077.

Bailey, Moya & Trudy. 2018. "On Misogynoir: Citation, Erasure, and Plagiarism," *Feminist Media Studies* 18, no. 3: 762–8.

Barnes, Katie. 2017. "Why 'The Bachelor' Franchise Isn't Ready for Another Black Lead," *ESPNW*, August 7, 2017 <http://www.espn.com/espnw/voices/article/20272223/why-bachelor-franchise-not-ready-another-black-lead>.

Benitez, Michael, Jr. 2010. "Resituating Culture Centers within a Social Justice Framework: Is There Room for Examining Whiteness?" in *Culture Centers in Higher Education: Perspectives on Identity, Theory, and Practice*, edited by Lori Patton (Sterling, VA: Stylus, 2010).

Berry, Daina R. 2016. "Nat Turner's Skull and My Student's Purse of Skin," *New York Times*, October 18, 2016.

Birnbaum, Emily. 2018. "Poll: More Than Half of Americans Can't Name a Single Supreme Court Justice," *The Hill*, August 28, 2018 <https://thehill.com/regulation/court-battles/403992-poll-more-than-half-of-americans-cant-name-single-supreme-court>.

Blaque, Kat. 2018. "What Is: Intersectionality," YouTube Video, January 9, 2018 <https://www.youtube.com/watch?v=lEeP_3vmdBY>.

Brown, Sherronda J. 2018a. "The Black Patriarchy Is Wrapped Up in the Dehumanization of Black Women," *Wear Your Voice*, December 10, 2018 <https://wearyourvoicemag.com/identities/black-patriarchy-black-women>.

——. 2018b. "Reading 'Black Museum' and 'Get Out' As Comparative Afrofuturist Zombie Slave Narratives," Black Youth Project, January 8, 2018 <http://blackyouthproject.com/reading-black-museum-get-comparative-afrofuturist-zombie-slave-narratives/>.

Buckwalter, Rebecca. 2014. "Judge Judy Is a National Treasure," *Pacific Standard*, February 20, 2014.

Butler, Anthea. 2015. "Shooters of Color are called 'Terrorists' and 'Thugs.' Why Are White Shooters Called 'Mentally Ill'?" *Washington Post*, June 18, 2015.

Byrne, Louise. 2017. "Isn't It Finally Time We Took Media Studies Seriously?" *Times Higher Education*, October 2, 2017.

Cherry Bomb. 2015. "Biko on 'White Allies' Place in the Struggle against Racism." *Fleurmach: Beyond Your Peripheral Vision*, March 23, 2015 <https://fleurmach.com/2015/03/23/biko-on-white-allies-place-in-the-struggle-against-racism/>. Originally from *I Write What I Like: Selected Writings of Steve Biko*, edited by Aelred Stubbs (Johannesburg: Heinemann, 1978).

Clegg, II, Legrand H. 2018. "How Lynching Was Used by Whites to Destroy Competition from Black Business Owners," *Los Angeles Times*, April 28, 2018.

Coates, Ta-Nehisi. "The Dubious Math Behind Stop and Frisk," *The Atlantic*, July 24, 2013.

Coles, Donyae. "8 Witches and Healers of Color to Follow Online," *Wear Your Voice*, July 22, 2017 <https://wearyourvoicemag.com/identities/healing-magick/8-witches-healers-color-follow-online>.

Cooney, Samantha. "Why People Are So Obsessed with *The Bachelor*, According to the Woman Who Wrote a Book on It," *TIME*, March 4, 2018.

Craven, Julia and K. Bellware. 2015. "We Weep for African Lions. But What about Black Lives?" *Huffington Post*, July 29, 2015 <https://www.huffingtonpost.com/entry/cecil-black-lives_us_55b9482ce4b095423d0dc4d5>.

Crenshaw, Kimberlé. 1989. "Demarginalizing the Intersection of Race and Sex: A Black Feminist Critique of Antidiscrimination Doctrine, Feminist Theory and Antiracist Politics," *University of Chicago Legal Forum* 140: 139–67.

Cruz, Lenika. 2017. "In *Get Out*, the Eyes Have It," *The Atlantic*, March 3, 2017.

Cullors, Patrisse. 2018. "On Trayvon Martin's Birthday, We Remember His Life and Why We Fight for Black Lives," *NBC News*, February 5, 2018 <https://www.nbcnews.com/think/opinion/trayvon-martin-s-birthday-we-remember-his-life-why-we-ncna844711>.

Curry, Tommy J. 2018a. "They Mistook a Backlash for a Movement: Black Men and the Doom of Western Civilization." YouTube Video, February 14, 2018 <https://www.youtube.com/watch?v=KtNhsGgEk54>.

——. 2018b. "Killing Boogeyman: Phallicism and the Misandric Mischaracterization of Black Males in Theory." *Res Philosophica* 95, no. 2: 235–72.

——. 2016. "'Eschatological Dilemmas: The Problem of Studying the Black Male only as the Deaths that Result from Anti-Black Racism," in *I Am Because We Are: Readings in African Philosophy*, edited by Fred Lee Hord and Jonathan Scott Lee, 2nd ed. (Amherst: University of Massachusetts Press, 2016), 479–99.

Da Costa, Cassie. 2017. "'Get Out' Captures Double Consciousness Perfectly," *Feministing*, March 15, 2017 <http://feministing.com/2017/03/15/feministing-films-get-out/>.

Daily Mail Reporter. 2015. "US Teens 'Had Three-way Sex on Corpses of Men They Lured to Their House, Strangled to Death and Hog-tied'," *Daily Mail*, May 28, 2015.

Dorsey, Avon. 2018. "Tiffany Haddish vs. PETA: 'When the Police Stop Killing Black People, I'll Stop Wearing Fur,'" *Essence*, December 30, 2018.

Du Bois, W. E. B. 1989. *The Souls of Black Folks*. New York: Penguin Classics.

Dubrofsky, Rachel. 2006. "*The Bachelor*: Whiteness in the Harem," *Critical Studies in Media Communication* 23, no. 1: 39–56.

Egelko, Bob. 2018. "SFPD Can Seek Discipline of Officers for Racist Texts," *San Francisco Chronicle*, September 12, 2018.

French, Megan. 2017. "'Bachelor' Alum Leah Block Under Fire for Racist 'Bachelorette' Comment: See Rachel Lindsay's Response." *US Weekly*, June 20, 2017.

Gambert, Iselin and Tobias Linne. 2018. "How the Alt-Right Uses Milk to Promote White Supremacy," *The Conversation*, April 26, 2018 <http://theconversation.com/how-the-alt-right-uses-milk-to-promote-white-supremacy-94854>.

Gardner, Eriq. 2012. "'The Bachelor' Racial Discrimination Lawsuit Dismissed," *Hollywood Reporter*, October 15, 2012.

Gayo, Loyce. 2017. "Sikiliza—There Is More to the Swahili Song in 'Get Out'," *Medium*, March 16, 2017 <https://medium.com/@loycegayo/sikiliza-there-is-more-to-the-swahili-song-in-get-out-79ebb1456116>.

Glave, Diane. 2010. *Rooted in the Earth: Reclaiming the African American Environmental Heritage*. Chicago: Chicago Review Press.

Gonzalez, Sandra. 2017. "For 'Bachelor' Viewers, the 'Absurdity' is the Fun," *CNN Entertainment*, March 14, 2017.

Gossett, Che. 2015. "Che Gossett: Blackness, Animality, and the Unsovereign." *Verso Books*, September 8, 2015 <https://www.versobooks.com/blogs/2228-che-gossett-blackness-animality-and-the-unsovereign>.

Gorski, Paul C. 2019. "Fighting Racism, Battling Burnout: Causes of Activist Burnout in US Racial Justice Activists," *Ethnic and Racial Studies* 42, no. 5: 667–87.

Gray, Jacquelyn. 2018. "Convict Who Had Sex on Murder Victims' Bodies Will Serve Less than Four Years Behind Bars," *Crime Online*, February 13, 2018 <https://www.crimeonline.com/2018/02/13/convict-who-had-sex-on-murder-victims-bodies-will-serve-less-than-four-years-behind-bars/>.

de Haldevang, Max. 2018. "Florida Shooter Nikolas Cruz Shared a Trait with Other Mass Killers: He Abused Women," *Quartz*, February 15, 2018 <https://qz.com/1208345/parkland-florida-attack-school-shooter-nikolas-cruz-abused-women-like-most-mass-killers/>.

Harris, Hunter. 2018. "Bachelor Creator Saw Low Ratings for Rachel Lindsay as 'Disturbing' and 'Trumpish.'" *Vulture*, January 26, 2018 <https://www.vulture.com/2018/01/bachelor-creator-on-ratings-dip-disturbing-trumpish.html>.

hooks, bell. 1989. "Straightening Our Hair" in *Talking Back: Thinking Feminist, Thinking Black*. Cambridge, MA: South End Press.

Hutchinson, Darren Lenard. 2001. "Identity Crisis: 'Intersectionality,' 'Multidimensionality,' and the Development of an Adequate Theory of Subordination," *Michigan Journal of Race and Law* 6: 285–317.

——. 1997. "Out Yet Unseen: A Racial Critique of Gay and Lesbian Legal Theory and Political Discourse," *Connecticut Law Review* 29, no. 2: 561–645.

International Slavery Museum, n.d. "Olaudah Equiano—Life on Board <http://www.liverpoolmuseums.org.uk/ism/slavery/middle_passage/olaudah_equiano.aspx>.

Jackson, Zakiyyah Iman. 2016. "Losing Manhood: Animality and Plasticity in the (Neo)Slave Narrative," *Critical Humanities and Social Sciences* 25, no. 1–2: 95–136.

Johnson, Lindgren. 2018. *Race Matters, Animal Matters: Fugitive Humanism in African America, 1840–1930*. New York: Routledge.

Johnson, T. Hasan. 2017. "Dr. T. Hasan Johnson at Texas A&M on Misandroir and Black Male Studies," *Black Masculinism and New Black Masculinities*, May 16, 2017 <https://newblackmasculinities.wordpress.com/2017/05/16/dr-t-hasan-johnson-at-texas-am-on-misandrior-and-black-male-studies/>.

——. 2015. "'Black Male Privilege in One Hand and Bull$#! in the Other, Which One Fills Up First?': Challenging the Myth of Black Male Privilege," *Black Masculinism and New Black Masculinities*, September 5, 2015 <https://newblackmasculinities.wordpress.com/2015/09/05/put-black-male-privilege-in-one-hand-and-bull-in-the-other-which-one-fills-up-first-by-t-hasan-johnson-ph-d/>.

Kay, Justin. Forthcoming, 2020. "Vegan-Washing Genocide: Animal Advocacy on Stolen Land and Re-imagining Animal Liberation as Anti-colonial Praxis," in *Anarchist Political Ecology: Undoing Human Supremacy*, edited by S. Springer, M. Locret-Collet, J. Mateer, J., and M. Acker <http://www.academia.edu/37656869/Vegan-Washing_Genocide_Animal_advocacy_on_stolen_land_and_re-imagining_animal_liberation_as_anti-colonial_praxis>.

Kim, Claire Jean. 2017. "Murder and Mattering in Harambe's House," *Politics and Animals* 3, no. 2: 37–51.

——. 2016. "Animals, Feminism, and Antiblackness." Unbound Project, October 31, 2016 <https://unboundproject.org/animals-feminism-and-antiblackness-2/>.

——. 2015. *Dangerous Crossings: Race, Species, and Nature in a Multicultural Age*. Cambridge, U.K.: Cambridge University Press.

Kirabo, Sincere. 2017. "Three Ways Black Veganism Challenges White Supremacy (Unlike Conventional Veganism)," *Black Youth Project*, October 23, 2017 <http://blackyouthproject.com/three-ways-black-veganism-challenges-white-supremacy-unlike-conventional-veganism/>.

Ko, Aph and Syl Ko. 2019. "Un-Disciplined: A Conversation between Two Sisters Who Left Graduate School," in *Counternarratives from Women of Color*

Academics: Bravery, Vulnerability, and Resistance, edited by Manya C. Whitaker and Eric Anthony Grollman (New York: Routledge, 2019).

——. 2017. *Aphro-ism: Essays on Pop Culture, Feminism, and Black Veganism from Two Sisters*. New York: Lantern Books.

Lang, Cady. 2018. "Jordan Peele Is Keeping His Oscar in the Most Horrifying Place Imaginable. Only *Get Out* Fans Will Recognize It," *TIME*, March 6, 2018 <http://time.com/5188033/jordan-peele-get-out-chair-oscars-2018/>.

Lartey, Jamiles and Sam Morris. 2018. "How White Americans Used Lynchings to Terrorize and Control Black People," *Guardian*, April 26, 2018.

Lee, Frances. 2017. "Excommunicate Me from the Church of Social Justice." *Autostraddle*, July 13, 2017 <https://www.autostraddle.com/kin-aesthetics-excommunicate-me-from-the-church-of-social-justice-386640/>.

Litwack, Leon. 2000. "Hellhounds," in *Without Sanctuary: Lynching Photography in America*, edited by J. Allen and J. Lewis (Santa Fe: Twin Palms Publishers, 2000).

Lugones, Maria. 2010. "Toward a Decolonial Feminism" *Hypatia* 25, no. 4: 742–59.

Lundblad, Michael. 2017. *Animalities: Literary and Cultural Studies beyond the Human*. Edinburgh: Edinburgh University Press.

Maningding, Ranier. 2017. "Why 'Get Out', A Movie about Anti-Black Racism, Had an Asian Character," *NextShark*, March 3, 2017 <https://nextshark.com/get-out-film-asian-character-racism-llag/>.

McIntosh, Peggy. 1988. "White Privilege and Male Privilege: A Personal Account of Coming to See Correspondences through Work in Women's Studies," Wellesley Centers for Women, Wellesley, MA <https://nationalseedproject.org/Key-SEED-Texts/white-privilege-and-male-privilege>.

McQuirter, Trayce. 2016. "Keep Eating for Activism." *By Any Greens Necessary*, July 13, 2016 <https://www.byanygreensnecessary.com/single-post/2016/07/13/Keep-Eating-for-Activism>.

Meraji, Shereen Marisol. 2015. "Outdoor Afro: Busting Stereotypes that Black People Don't Hike or Camp," *NPR*, July 12, 2015 <https://www.npr.org/sections/codeswitch/2015/07/12/421533481/outdoor-afro-busting-stereotypes-that-blacks-dont-hike-or-camp>.

Mignolo, Walter. 2011. "Epistemic Disobedience and the Decolonial Option: A Manifesto," *Transmodernity: Journal of Peripheral Cultural Production of the Luso-Hispanic World* I, no. 2: 44–66.

Molina, Brett. 2018. "Cashing Checks, Napping, More Activities Leading to Police Calls on Black People in 2018," *USA Today*, December 20, 2018.

Moore, Donald, J. Kosek, and A. Pandian. 2003. "Introduction: The Cultural Politics of Race and Nature: Terrains of Power and Practice," in *Race, Nature and the Politics of Difference*, edited by D. S. Moore, J. Kosek, and A. Pandian (Durham, N.C.: Duke University Press, 2003).

Mutua, Athena D. 2013. "Multidimensionality Is to Masculinities What Intersectionality Is to Feminism," *Nevada Law Journal* 13, no. 341: 341–67.

——. 2012. "The Multidimensional Turn: Revisiting Progressive Black Masculinities in Multidimensional Masculinities and Law: Feminist Theory Meets Critical Race Theory," available at SSRN <https://papers.ssrn.com/sol3/papers.cfm?abstract_id=2104406>.

Nathman, Avital N. 2013. "The Femisphere: Foodies and Food Politics," *Ms.*, March 12, 2013 <http://msmagazine.com/blog/2013/03/12/the-femisphere-foodies-and-food-politics/>.

Nduaguba, Adaeze. 2017. "Feminist Guide to *Get Out*," *Dartmouth*, May 24, 2017 <https://journeys.dartmouth.edu/feministguidetogetout/2017/05/24/cotton-chair/>.

Nott, Josiah, and George R. Gliddon. 1854. *Types of Mankind or Ethnological Researches, Based upon the Ancient Monuments, Paintings, Sculptures, and Crania of Races.* Kessinger Legacy Reprints. See <https://archive.org/details/typesofmankindor00nott/page/n8>.

Obeidallah, Dean. 2018. "Nikolas Cruz Was a Racist. Does that Make His Attack Terrorism?" *Daily Beast*, March 1, 2018 <https://www.thedailybeast.com/nikolas-cruz-was-a-racist-does-that-make-his-attack-terrorism>.

Perkinson, James W. 2005. *Shamanism, Racism, and Hip Hop Culture: Essays on White Supremacy and Black Subversion.* New York: Palgrave Macmillan.

——. 2004. "Reversing the Gaze: Constructing European Race Discourse as Modern Witchcraft Practice," *Journal of the American Academy of Religion* 72, no. 3: 603–29.

Pires, Candice. 2018. "'Bad Things Happen in the Woods': The Anxiety of Hiking While Black," *Guardian*, July 13, 2018.

Politi, Daniel. 2018. "Protestors Trash H&M Shops in South Africa Following Racist Ad," *Slate*, January 13, 2018 <https://slate.com/news-and-politics/2018/01/protesters-trash-h-and-m-shops-in-south-africa-following-racist-ad.html>.

Ramos, Reniel Rodríguez. 2014. "The Anthropological Consumption of Non-Human Primates, the Other Black Meat, Life," *The Excitement of Biology 2*, no. 1: 2–12.

Rose, Georgia. 2014. "Meeting the Cannibal Tribes of Indonesian New Guinea," *Vice*, December 4, 2014 <https://www.vice.com/en_us/article/qbe55p/hanging-out-with-cannibals-georgia-rose-377>.

Rosenberg, Alyssa. 2017. "'Get Out' Captures How White Supremacy Isolates Black People Even from Each Other," *Washington Post*, March 15, 2017.

Ruffin, Kimberly N. 2010. *Black on Earth: African American Ecoliterary Traditions*. Athens: University of Georgia Press.

Runk, Julie Velásquez, Chindío Peña Ismare, and Toño Peña Conquista. 2019. "Animal Transference and Transformation Among Wounann," *Journal of Latin American and Caribbean Anthropology* <https://anthrosource.onlinelibrary.wiley.com/doi/full/10.1111/jlca.12389>.

Samuel, Sigal. 2018. "The Witches of Baltimore," *The Atlantic*, November 5, 2018.

Sen, Satadru. 2010. *Savagery and Colonialism in the Indian Ocean: Power, Pleasure, and the Andaman Islands*. London: Routledge.

Shear, Michael D., and Eileen Sullivan. 2018. "Trump Calls Omarosa Manigualt Newman 'That Dog' in His Latest Insult," *New York Times*, August 14, 2018.

Smith, Kimberly. 2007. *African American Environmental Thought: Foundations*. Lawrence: University Press of Kansas.

Smith, Zadie. 2017. "Getting In and Out: Who Owns Black Pain?" *Harper's*, July 2017.

Sollee, Kristen J. 2017. *Witches, Sluts, Feminists: Conjuring the Sex Positive*. Berkeley: ThreeL Media.

Sumner, William G. 1907. *Folkways: A Study of the Sociological Importance of Usages, Manners, Customs, Mores, and Morals*. Boston: Ginn and Company.

Turner, Martha Warry. 2012. "Hiding, Hunting, and Habitat: An Environmental Re-Analysis of the Slave Narratives," Boise State

University Thesis <https://scholarworks.boisestate.edu/cgi/viewcontent.cgi?article=1304&context=td>.

Vanity Fair. 2017. "Jordan Peele Breaks Down 'Get Out' Fan Theories from Reddit," YouTube Video, December 1, 2017 <https://www.youtube.com/watch?v=hBvcngHRTFg>.

VeganLife. 2017. "Black Vegans Rock—Aph Ko Talks about Her Remarkable Work," *VeganLife* magazine, April 3, 2017 <https://www.veganlifemag.com/black-vegans-rock/>.

VILDA Team. 2019. "A Conversation on Diversity in Veganism with Writer Aph Ko," *VILDA* magazine, January 18, 2019 <http://www.vildamagazine.com/2019/01/diversity-in-veganism/>.

Wakeham, Pauline. 2008. *Taxidermic Signs: Reconstructing Aboriginality.* Minneapolis: University of Minnesota Press.

Walsten, Jessika. 2017. "Syndication Ratings: 'Judge Judy' Wins May 2017 Sweep," *Broadcasting Cable,* June 7, 2017 <https://www.broadcastingcable.com/news/syndication-ratings-judge-judy-wins-may-2017-sweep-166357>.

Wear Your Voice. 2017. "Here's Why Witches of Color Are Gathering in Washington D.C. on the Anniversary of the 2017 Inauguration," *Wear Your Voice,* November 7, 2017 <https://wearyourvoicemag.com/identities/heres-witches-color-gathering-anniversary-2017-inauguration>.

Womack, Ytasha. 2013. *Afrofuturism: The World of Black Sci-Fi and Fantasy Culture.* Chicago: Chicago Review Press.

Woodard, Vincent. 2014. *The Delectable Negro: Human Consumption and Homoeroticism within US Slave Culture.* New York: New York University Press.

Wright, Laura. 2018. "Introducing Vegan Studies," *ISLE: Interdisciplinary Studies in Literature and Environment* 24, no. 4: 727–36.

Yamato, Jen. 2017. "Jordan Peele Explains 'Get Out's' Creepy Milk Scene, Ponders the Recent Link Between Dairy and Hate," *Los Angeles Times,* March 21, 2017.

Young, Damon. 2016. "Hotep, Explained," *The Root,* March 5, 2016 <https://www.theroot.com/hotep-explained-1790854506>.

Young, Harvey. 2005. "The Black Body as Souvenir in American Lynching." *Theatre Journal* 57, no. 4: 639–57.

ACKNOWLEDGMENTS

THANK YOU TO MY HUSBAND, WES, FOR BEING SUPPORTIVE AND WORKING around my writing. Thanks for believing in me, supporting me, and always encouraging me to share my voice unapologetically. You are the one person who holds me together and I will forever love you. You are so incredibly insightful and intelligent, and I appreciate your labor. You took time to listen to me work out ideas, and you even helped me say things in new and different ways. You also dragged me when certain concepts didn't make sense, or if obvious gaps were present in the theory. I am forever grateful for your mind. I love you.

Thanks to Martin Rowe and Emily Lavieri-Scull at Lantern Books. Thank you for always believing in my projects and supporting me in my journey to share my thoughts and words with the public. I can't thank you enough for your encouragement and your unconditional support. You have changed my life by publishing thoughts that I would have probably kept hidden forever.

Thanks to Alise and Jack at EastRand Studios. I'm *so lucky* to work with you. You both continually capture my imagination! You are very talented and I can't wait to see what we work on next!

Thanks to close friends who have supported me throughout this arduous journey: lauren Ornelas, Alissa Hauser, Meghan Lowery, Breeze Harper, Jasmin Singer, Pax Ahimsa Gethen, and Lisa Spinazola (thank you so much for sending me article after article. I couldn't have written this book without your help). Other people I would like to thank include: Aaron Gross, Ytasha Womack, Tananarive Due, Jamie Broadnax, James Perkinson, Laura Wright, Lindgren Johnson, Nichole & Callie, and Pierce

Delahunt. Thank you to Jim Greenbaum, Dr. Bronner's, A Well-Fed World, and Animal Charity Evaluators for funding my work. Thank you to Hanh Nguyen for copyediting this book.

Claire Jean Kim—thank you for contributing to this book and keeping me calm and relaxed throughout the process. I appreciate your check-ins throughout my pregnancy! I don't think you realize how revolutionary your scholarship is to the public. Thank you for your mind.

Thanks to brilliant scholars and activists whose words have inspired me: Tommy Curry, Che Gosset, Zakiyyah Jackson, Rachel Dubrofsky, Aisha Durham, Vincent Woodard, and T. Hasan Johnson. This book wouldn't have been a possibility if brilliant thinkers didn't lay down the framework for me to use to create some of my own ideas.

Thank you to Jordan Peele for creating a film that served as the fuel for me to keep writing about these subjects. *Get Out* reminds me of why I studied media studies!

Thanks to my family for always loving and supporting me.

Thank you to the readers who care enough to open the book in the first place. Thank you for going on this journey with me as I try to find different theoretical ways to comment on current oppressions. I hope my thoughts help you articulate your own. This book wouldn't be a reality without your support.

Also, thanks to my baby girl, who provided me with inspiration to continue to write and to stop letting self-doubt take over this entire experience. The contractions I experienced while completing this book served as a reminder of how important it is to contribute and change the world for the next generation. You are my heart and my love. I hope you read this in the future and feel proud.

About the Author

APH KO is a writer and indie digital media producer. She is the founder of Black Vegans Rock and co-author of *Aphro-ism: Essays on Pop Culture, Feminism, and Black Veganism from Two Sisters*. Aph also served as the Associate Producer for the documentary *Always in Season*, which won the U.S. Documentary Special Jury award for Moral Urgency at the Sundance Film Festival in 2019.

ABOUT THE PUBLISHER

LANTERN BOOKS was founded in 1999 on the principle of living with a greater depth and commitment to the preservation of the natural world. In addition to publishing books on animal advocacy, vegetarianism, religion, and environmentalism, Lantern is dedicated to printing books in the US on recycled paper and saving resources in day-to-day operations. Lantern is honored to be a recipient of the highest standard in environmentally responsible publishing from the Green Press Initiative.

lanternbooks.com